SACRED
SPACE

SACRED SPACE
PINE HOLLOW

LESLIE LEE

LESLIE LEE PUBLISHER
TRAVERSE CITY, MICHIGAN

© 2014 Leslie Lee

All rights reserved. No part of this publication may be reproduced, stored in a retrieval system, or transmitted in any form or by any means electronic, mechanical, photocopying, recording or otherwise, without the prior written permission of the publisher.

Published by
Leslie Lee Publisher
Traverse City, Michigan

Publisher's Cataloging-in-Publication Data
Lee, Leslie.

Sacred space : Pine Hollow / Leslie Lee. – Traverse City, MI :
Leslie Lee Publisher, 2014.

   p. ; cm.

   ISBN13: 978-0-9915022-0-2

   1. Pine Hollow Institute. 2. Country homes—Michigan—Elk Rapids. 3. Architectural design.
   4. Architecture—Poetry. 5. Poetry I. Title.

NA7561.L44 2014
728.37—dc23   2014904430

Project coordination by Jenkins Group, Inc. • www.BookPublishing.com

Photography by
Jon Miller and Jeff Millies of Hedrich Blessing Photographers, Ltd., in Chicago, Illinois
Nancy Crafts Photography in Sausalito, California
Ken Scott Photography in Suttons Bay, Michigan

Cover and Interior design by Leslie Lee
Layout by Yvonne Fetig Roehler
Composed in Myriad Pro

Printed in the United States of America
18　17　16　15　14　•　5　4　3　2　1

For all the grandchildren

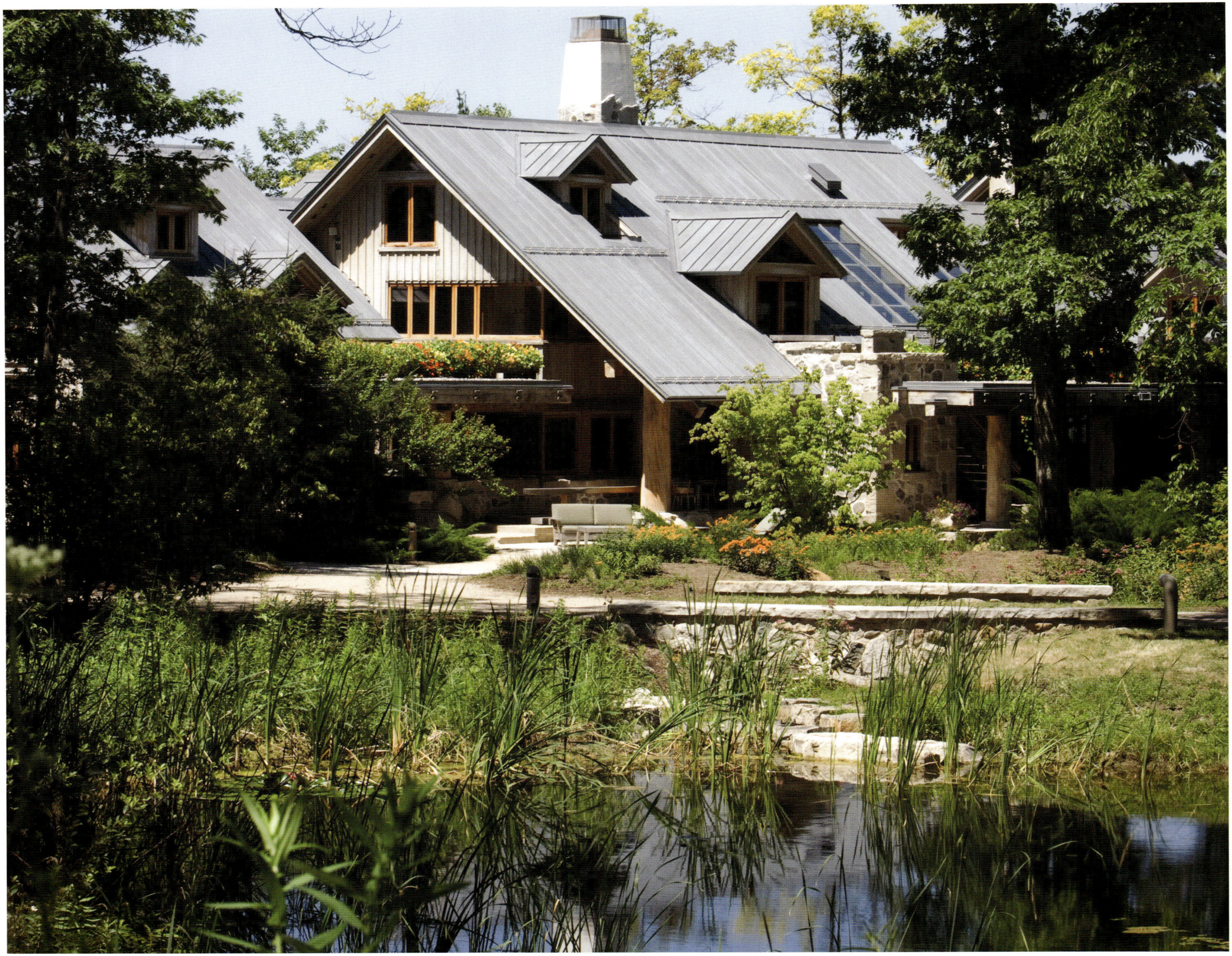

PINE HOLLOW

I find my way back through memory to explain how Pine Hollow came to be. I suppose, like a house, with the foundation. It began with love. The wellspring of this has been the deep appreciation of my extended family, my origins and my profound sense of belonging to the lakes and landscapes of Northwest Lower Michigan.

From the beginning, I decided to build Pine Hollow with local materials to last a thousand years. That, and the esthetic that it would be welcoming, elegant, strong, charming, and authentic, directed its design and construction. The foundation is massive. The walls are thirteen inches of load-bearing local granite and limestone, with Michigan white oak timber posts and beams, glacier-scraped limestone floors, a zinc roof, and honest, enduring materials and finishes throughout. I have called it a *vernacular architecture* because it is the embodiment of the geography and climate of our region's fundamental elements.

After two years of planning and design with architect Roger A. Hummel, we teamed with Comstock Construction Company as the construction manager. As a triad, we led the project. It took seven years of active building by our team with hundreds of the area's finest craftsmen to complete the structure. As we worked, we began to understand that we were taking part in a creation that was not only about us, but would be a force felt into the distant years. It would be for our grandchildren, for their grandchildren, and for the unknown. It created an attitude of striving for excellence, rather than striving to acquire and occupy a possession.

In 1996, I decided I needed a larger purpose to inspire its completion. Rather than build for my personal family, we began to work for the world as family and put our efforts toward the benefit of all life on Earth. The house embodies our dreams for a better future. We have built a house as fine as humanly possible to last the ages in honor of the natural world we share. For those of us who worked here, we have had the opportunity and gratification of working as a team using our intelligence, problem solving, and creativity in this shared experience of a lifetime. Our combined efforts have enriched my life immeasurably.

Pine Hollow graces a site of great natural beauty—beginning at the farm gate, the lane winds through a meadow of Michigan prairie, past the organic kitchen garden and orchard, and in seven acres, offers much of the region's native horticulture in its woodland, streams, waterfall, ponds, dunes, and 600 feet of Lake Michigan shoreline. The landscape was designed to lower the blood pressure and to raise the energy by returning the grounds to a native state that encourages each of us to reconnect with our own imperishable soul. Pine Hollow is a place to create, to learn, to heal and to live together in peace. It is a metaphor as a dwelling for the world. I share it with you as the Pine Hollow Institute.

Thank you, welcome home.

Leslie Lee

SACRED SPACE

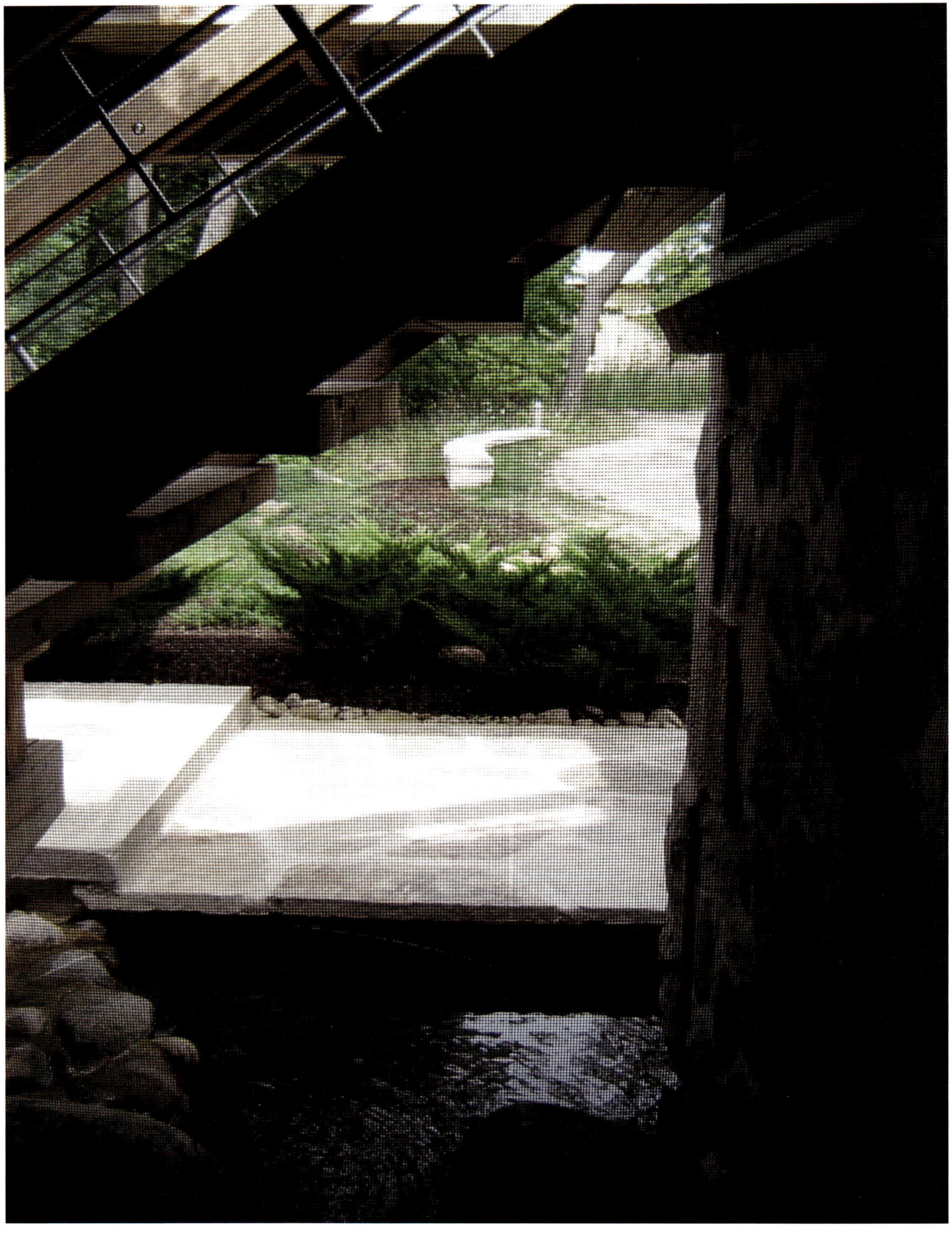

PLACE

My memories are home in humble silence here

as scents of sea arise from limestone walls on days

of rain like this.

I still can smell crustaceous salt

and pause in reverie as images of life

remind me of ancestral versions of myself.

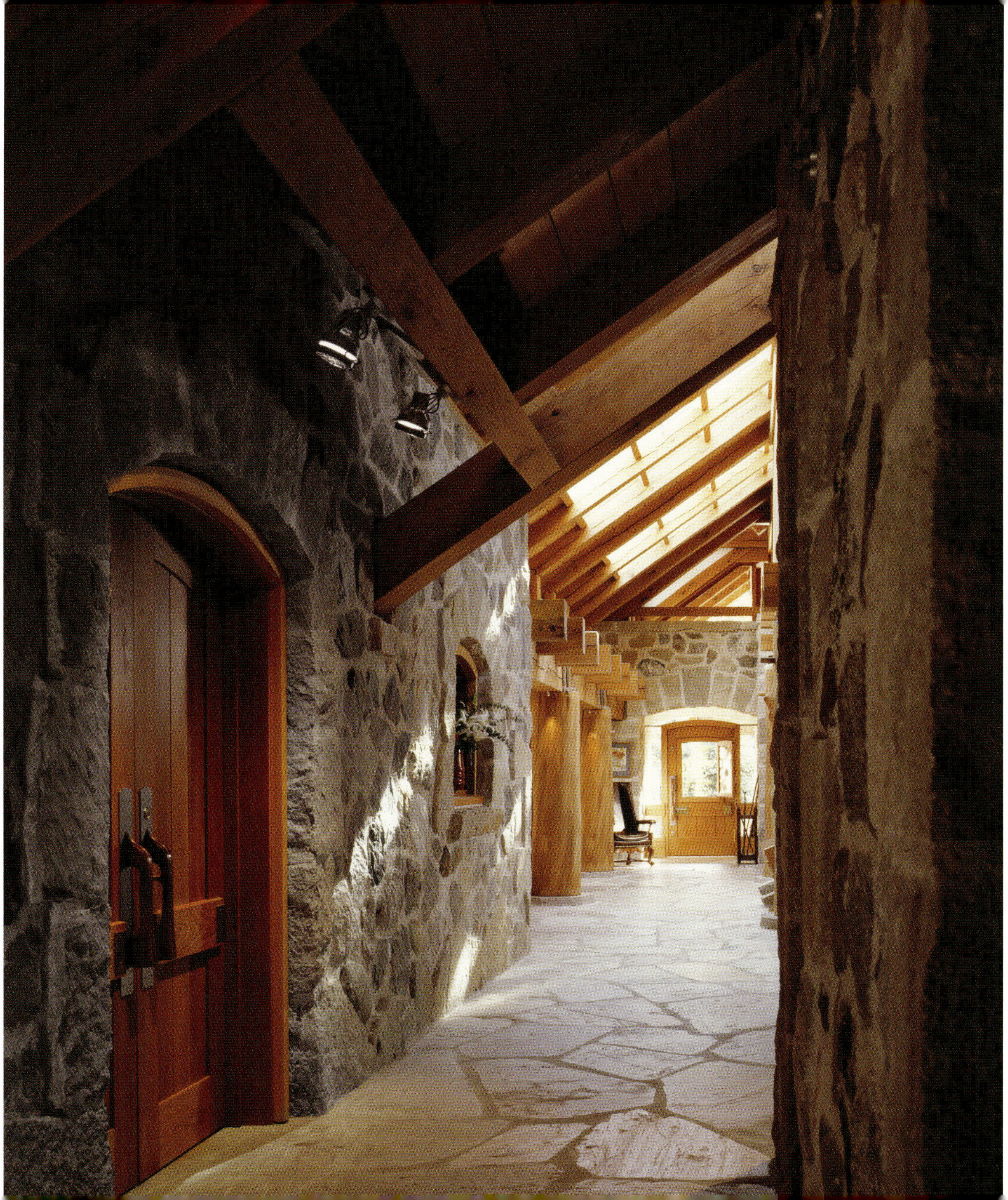

photo ©KenScottPhotography.com

I saw an ancient line of mountains in the North

arise from molten pools inside an airless world,

and seams of copper cool in Canada's granite,

and algae bloom a billion years of oxygen

into the toxic soup of atmosphere on Earth.

Tectonic forces shifted surface crusts from one

or other latitude while greenery exhaled

enriching air for tiny creatures living there,

and larger ones that fed off reefs of coral beds

in equatorial oceans that flowed offshore.

photo ©KenScottPhotography.com

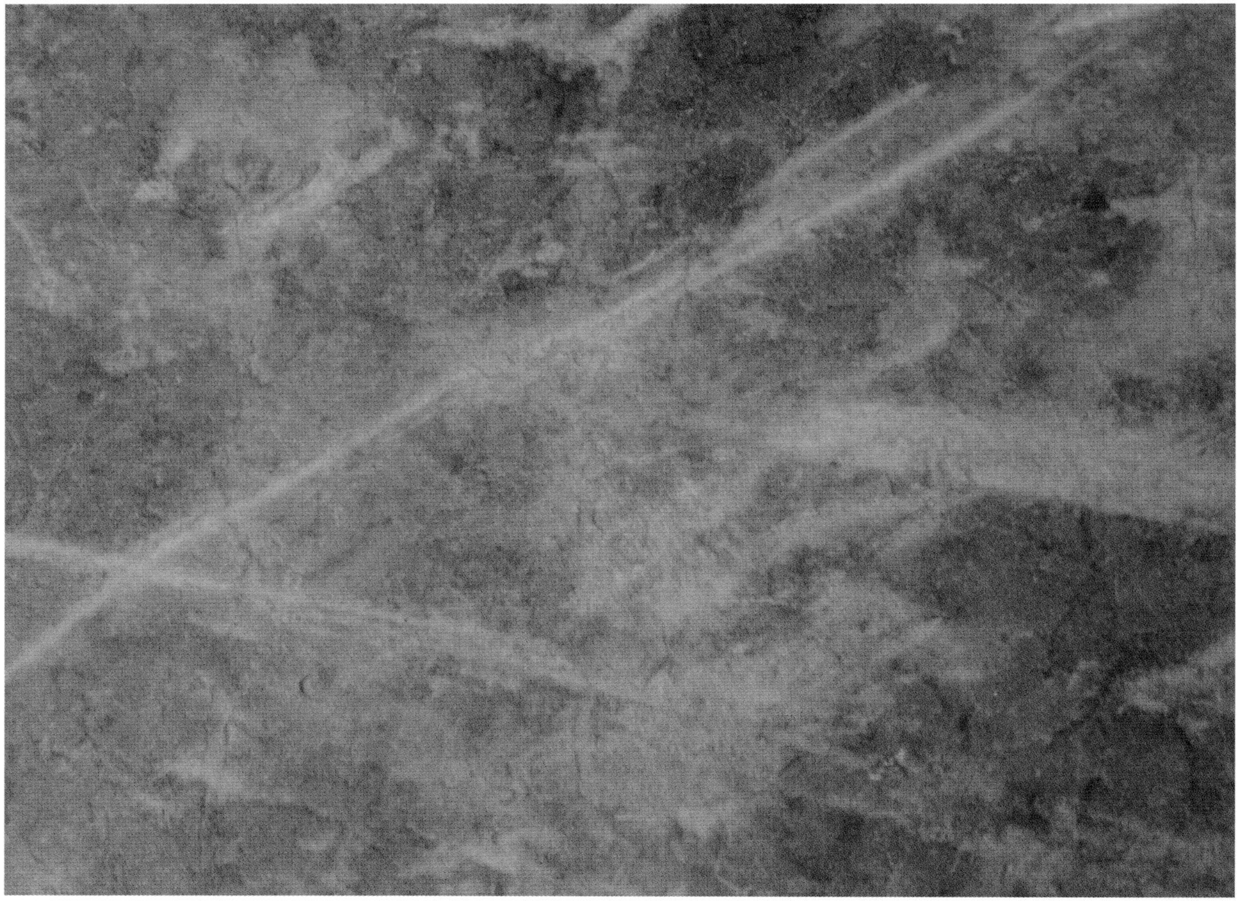

Impenetrable ice, ten thousand years ago,

a mile above the lake it left in its retreat,

inscribed a polished passage on the former bed

of ocean life still etched upon this stony floor,

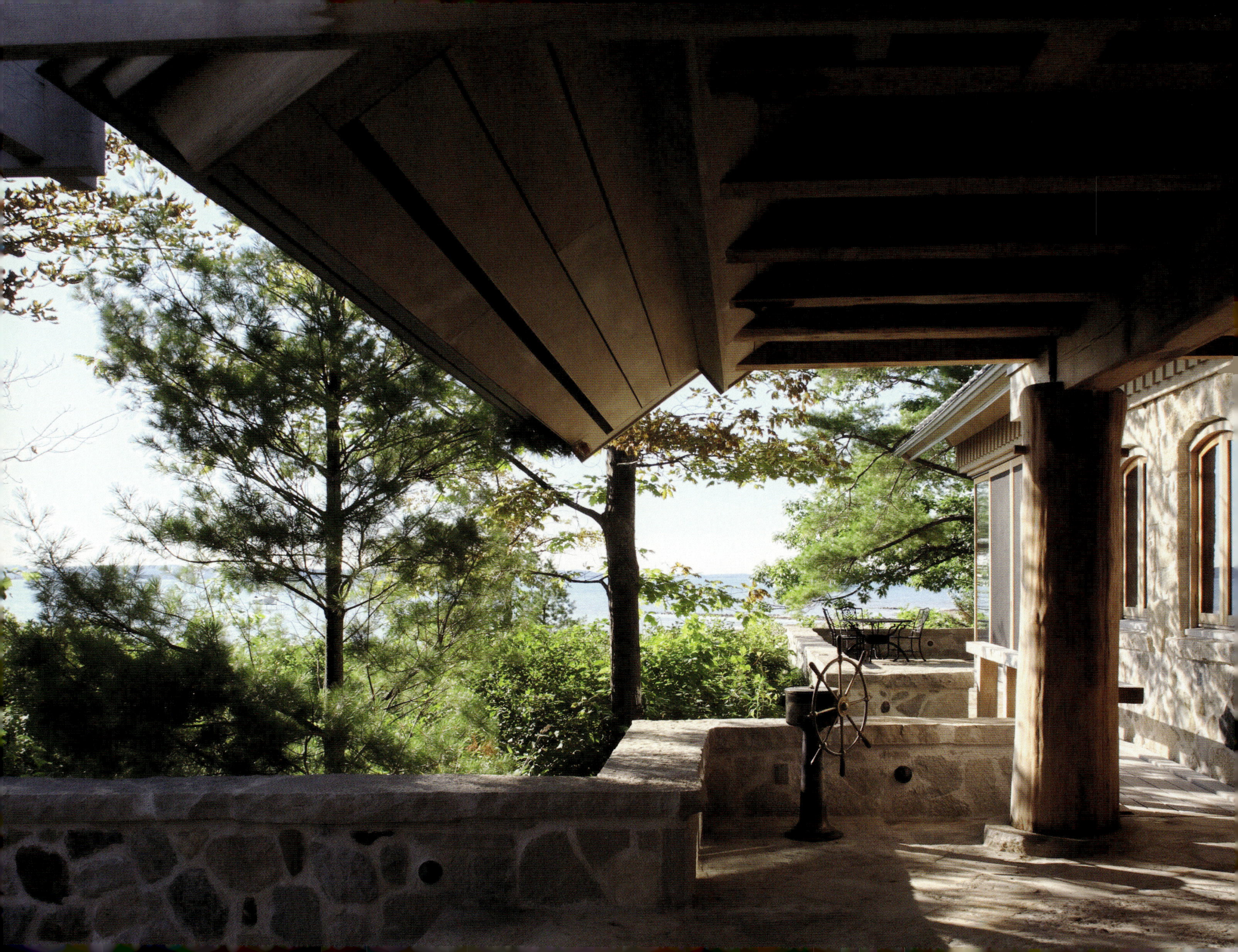

and deeper still, carved lakes
that filled with glacial melt.

The mammoths grazed on tundra grass before the trees

took root, and people followed with their fire and tools

by coast into the russet warmth of setting suns.

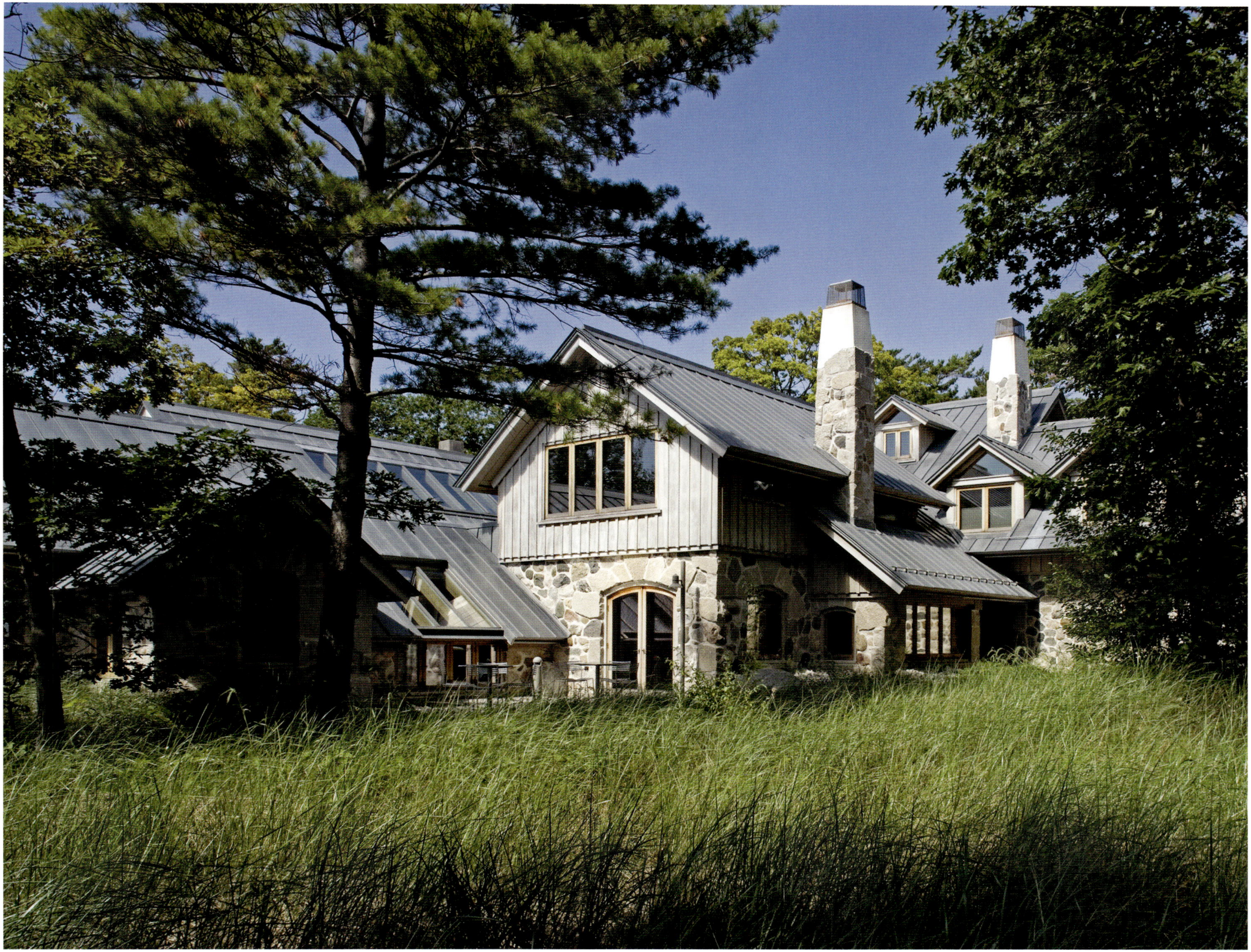

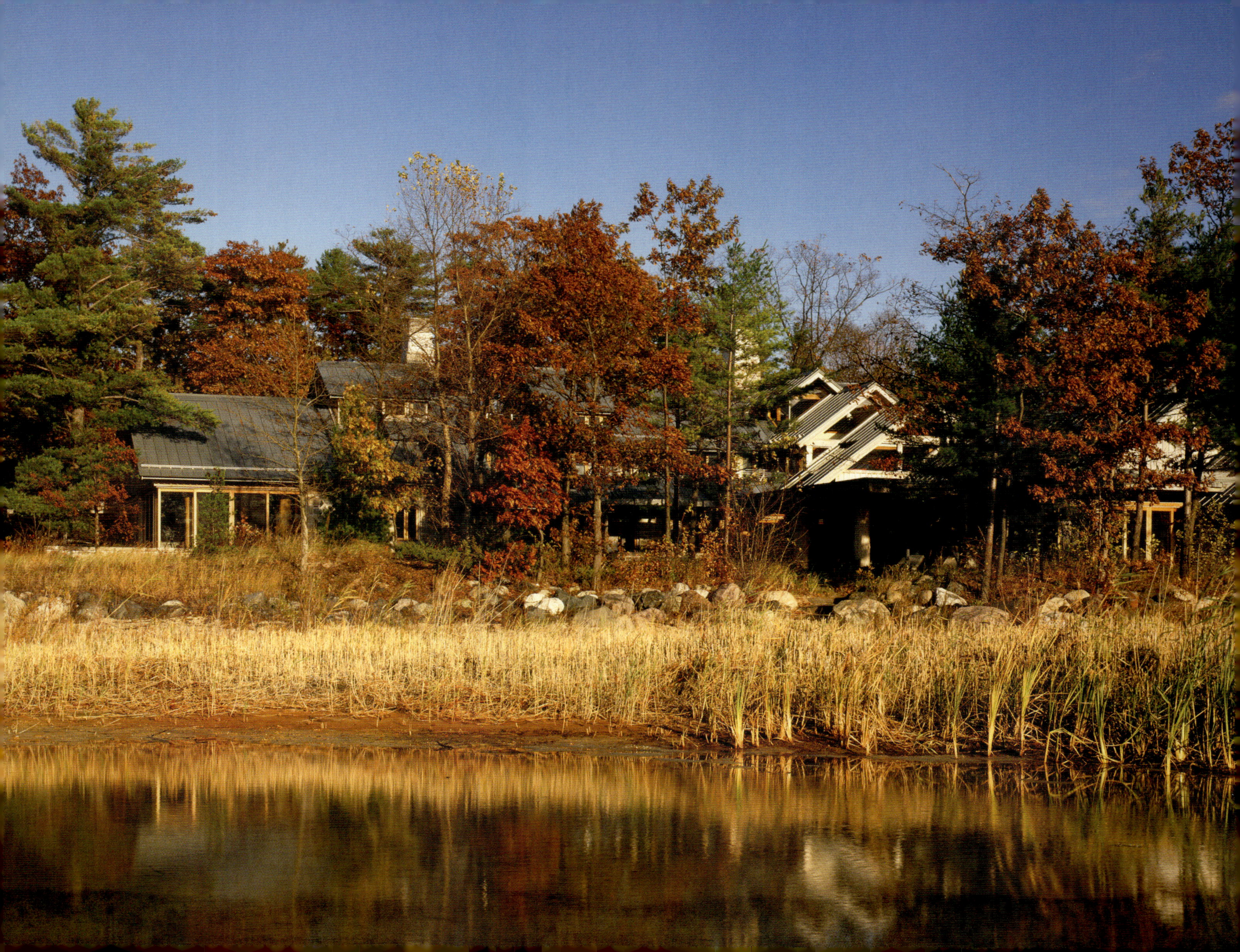

Here, eras of geology sit side by side—

ephemeral edges where the human dreams begin.

photo ©KenScottPhotography.com

An ancient soul united with this sacred place

beneath the stars, inside the wind, within the lake.

The voices of my childhood songs and stories form

the fundamental chord of this bequeathed refrain

with harmonies to echo on a thousand years.

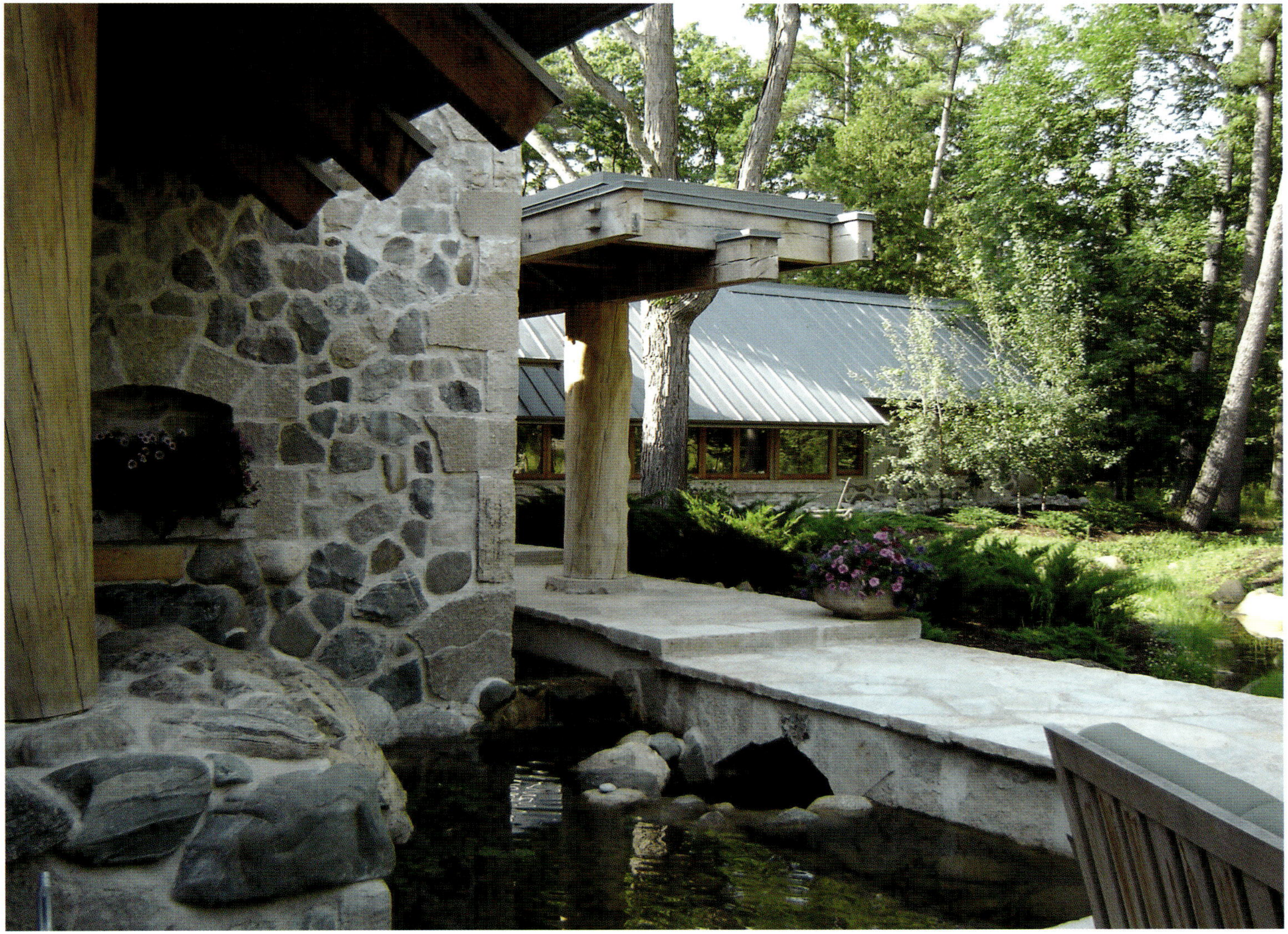

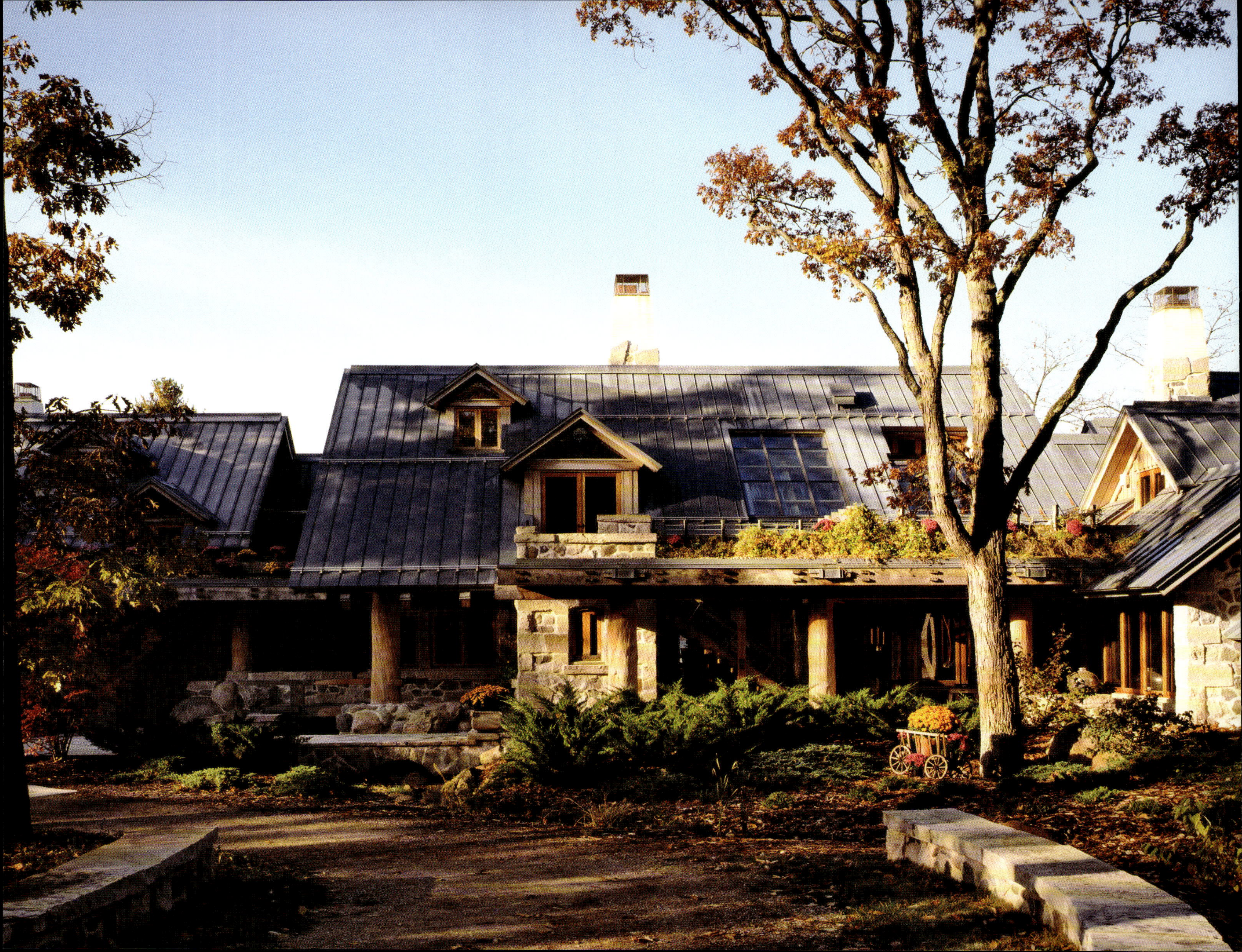

STRUCTURE

A white oak tree beside the creek, roots deep in soil,

then pillars up, with mirrored branches arching out

to bind the shadows of the Earth to heaven's sun.

It lives along a row of comrades cut for life,

their spirits born anew by human will to build.

The strength of oak, longevity of teak, cast brass

and hardened steel transformed by hand to timber frame.

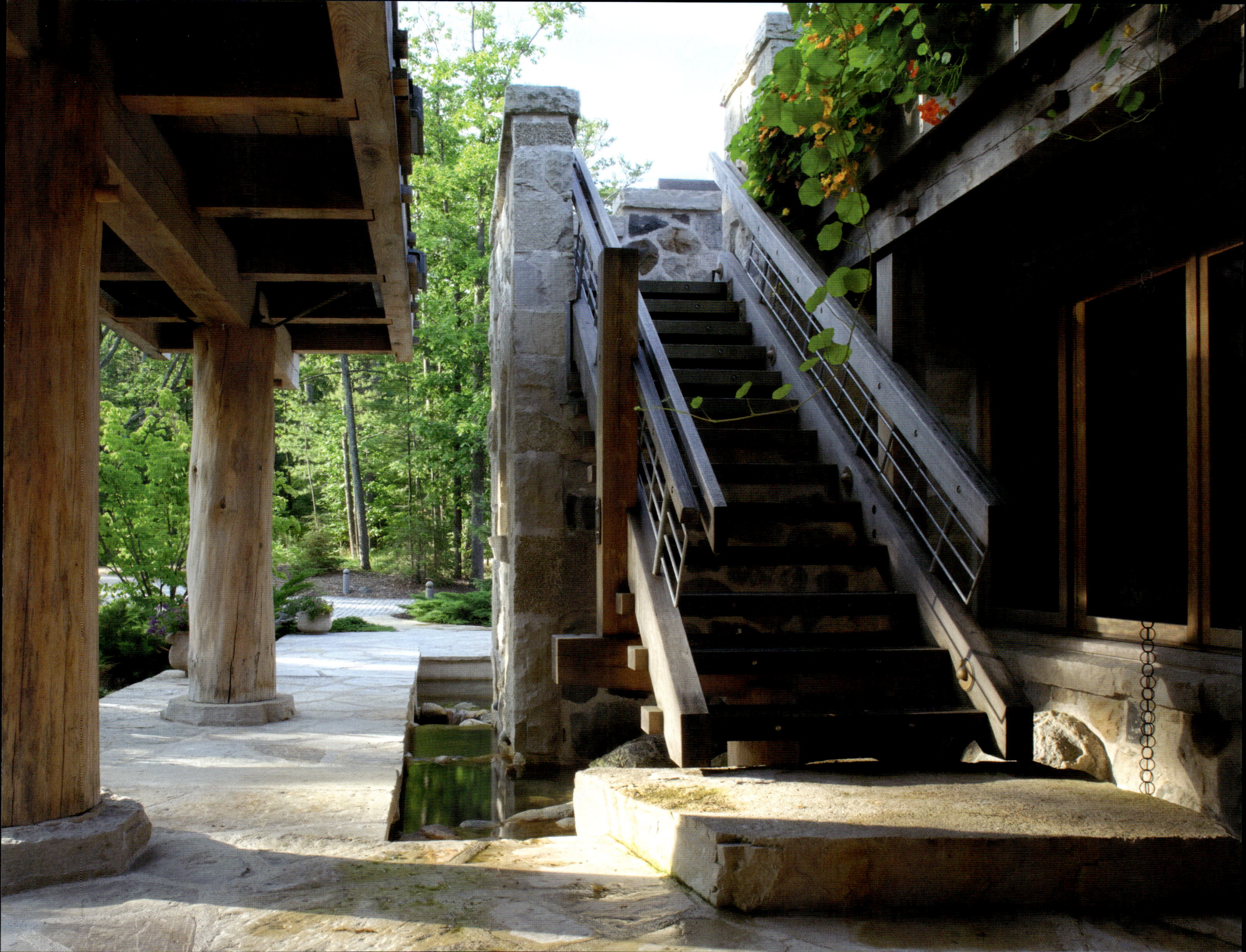

The rocks, once strewn in fields, now tightly packed, uphold

the rolled and folded zinc of water-shedding roof.

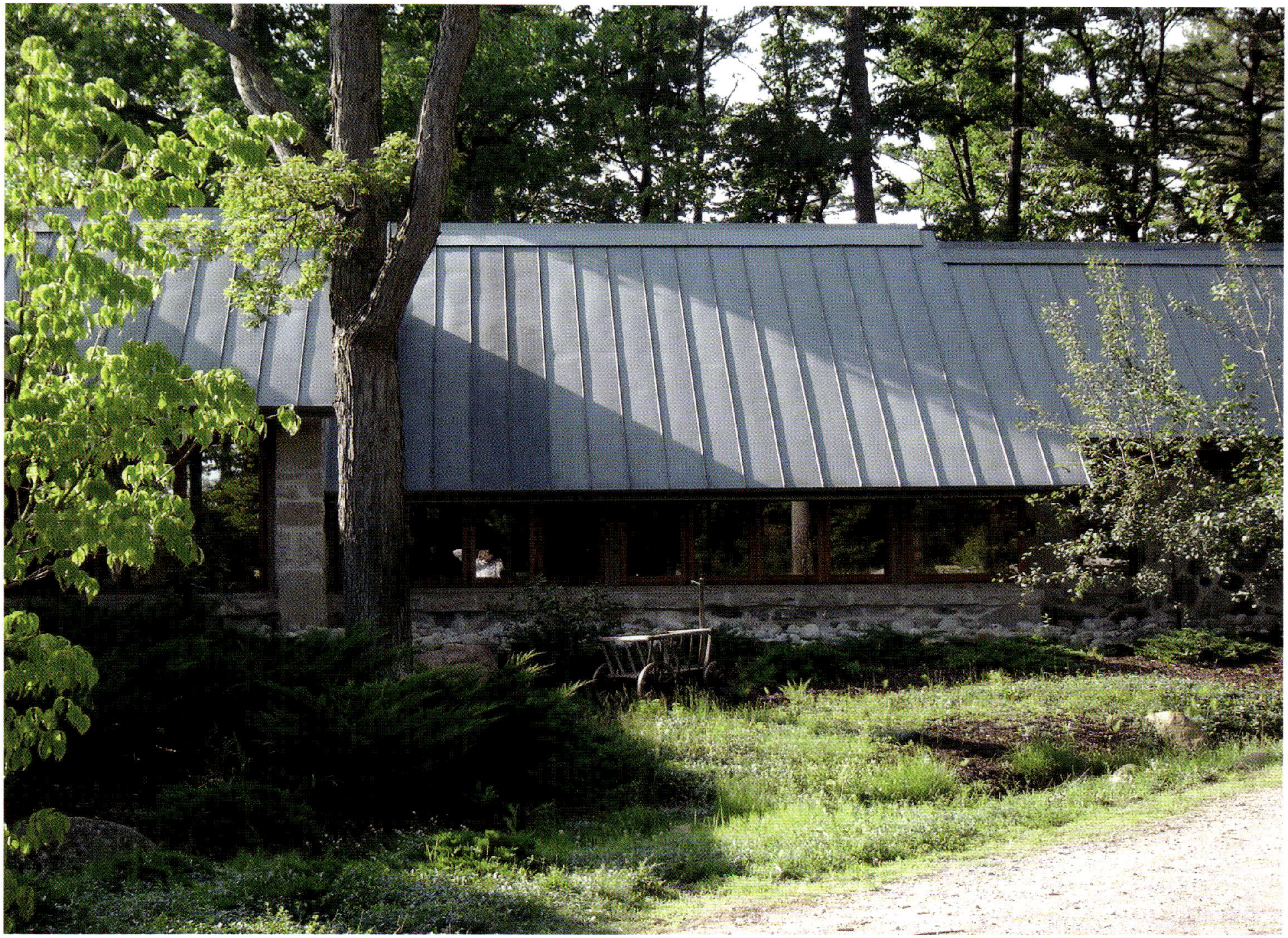

Here, textures raw in life shine with the craft of men.

The unity of post and beam supports the group

of smaller family members notched into the walls,

those voluntary limits that define the frame.

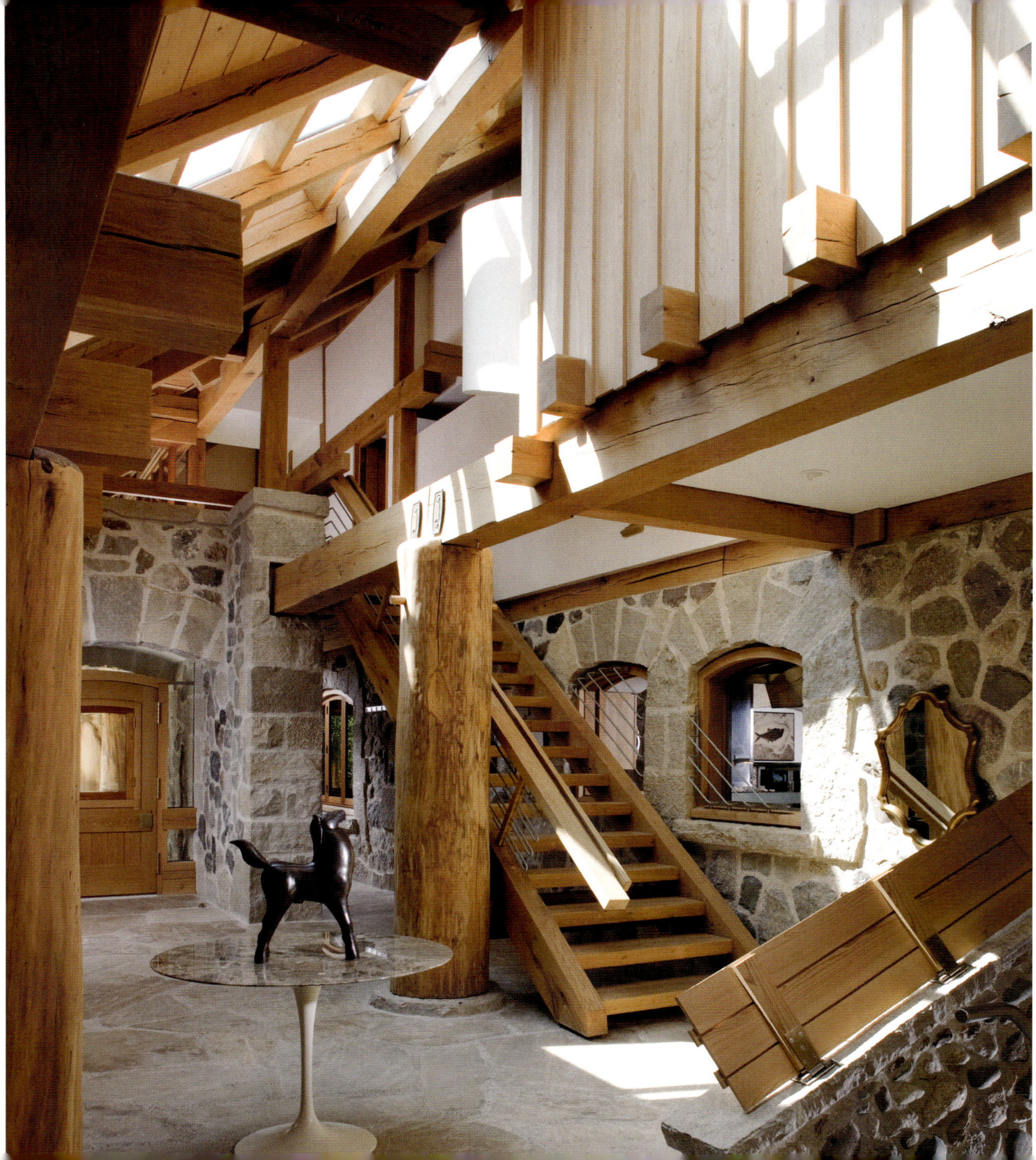

The boundaries, of *this I am, and that I'm not*

construct the character, diversity and form.

The structure leaps and soars from roof to walls as if

to prove it moves alone from one plane to the next,

cascading risks that skip from eaves down to the floor

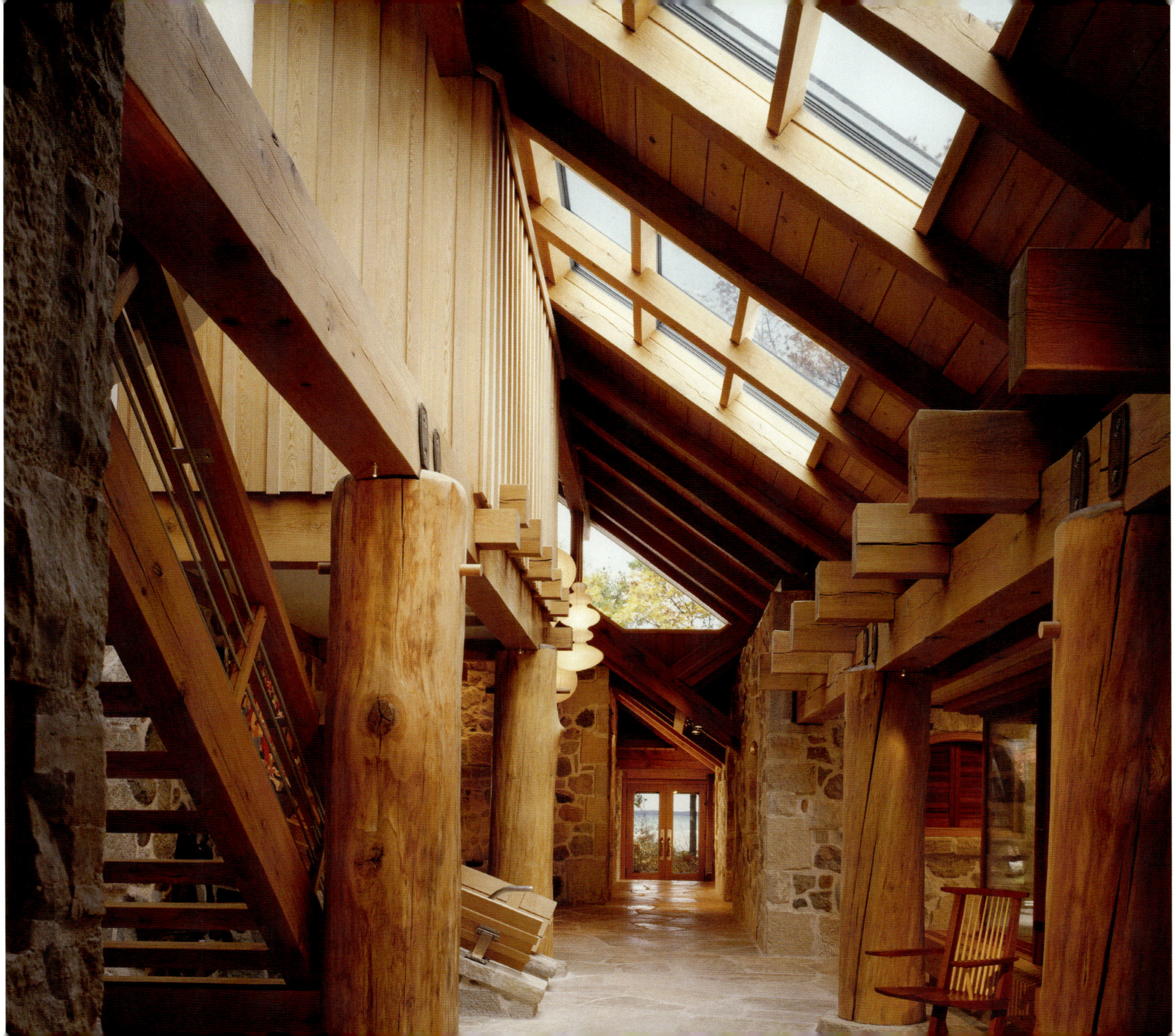

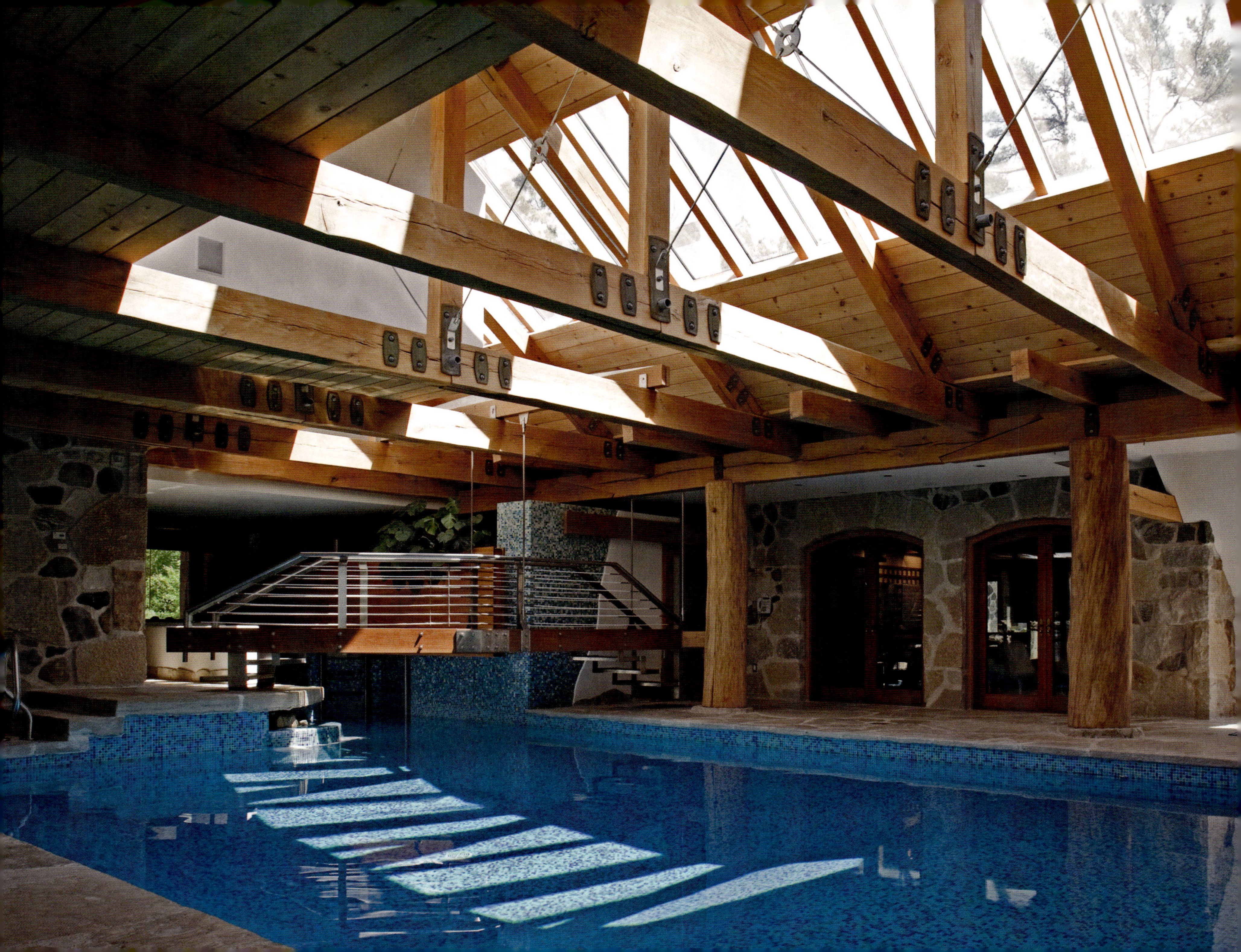

in steps so small that no one could object to such

a major shift in so small a space and short a time.

It tiptoes through the ancient streets and courtyards

of an older world to peer into the heart of home—

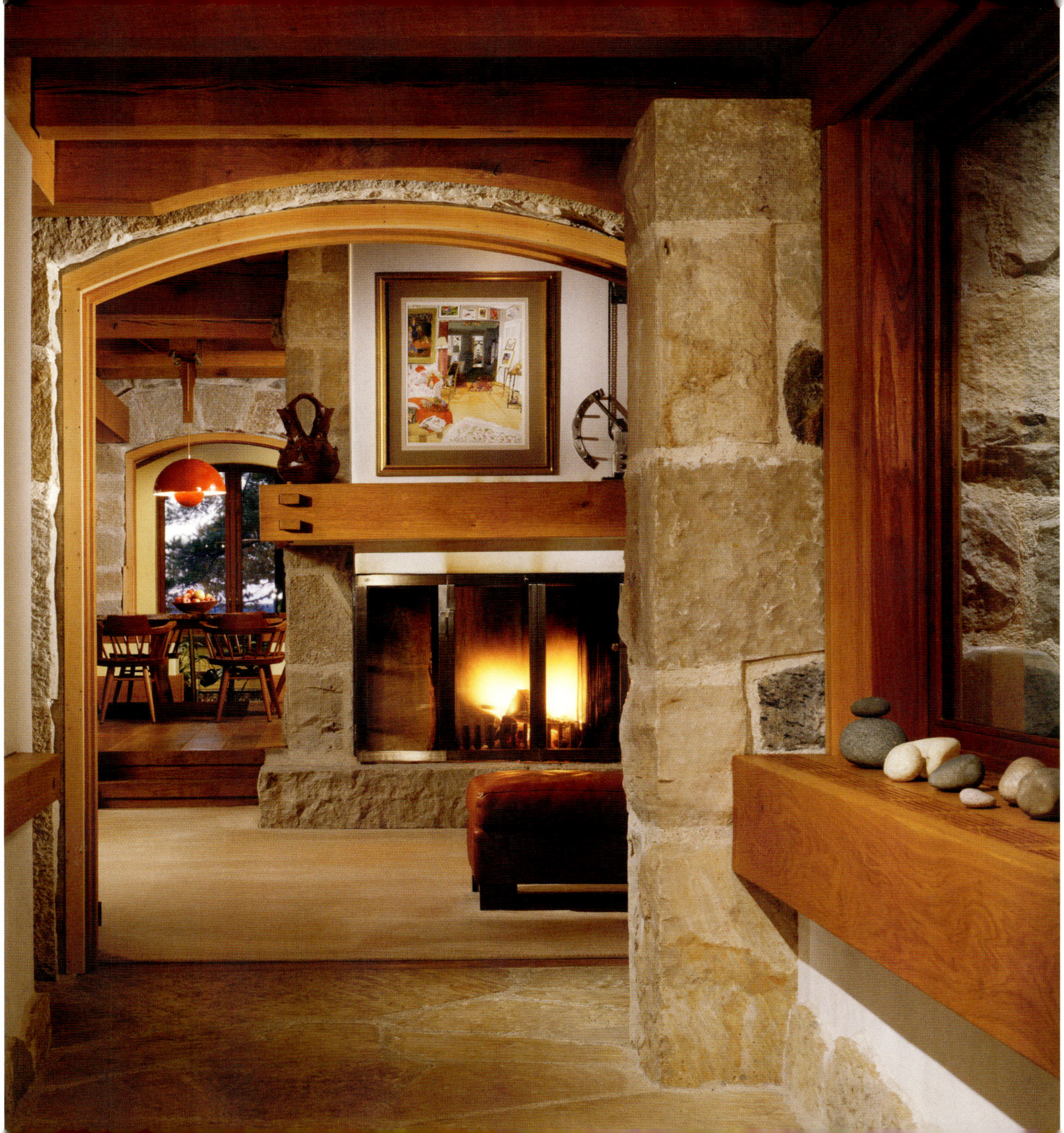

the single room of hearth and fire, of food and drink,

of songs and tales and family safe from stormy seas.

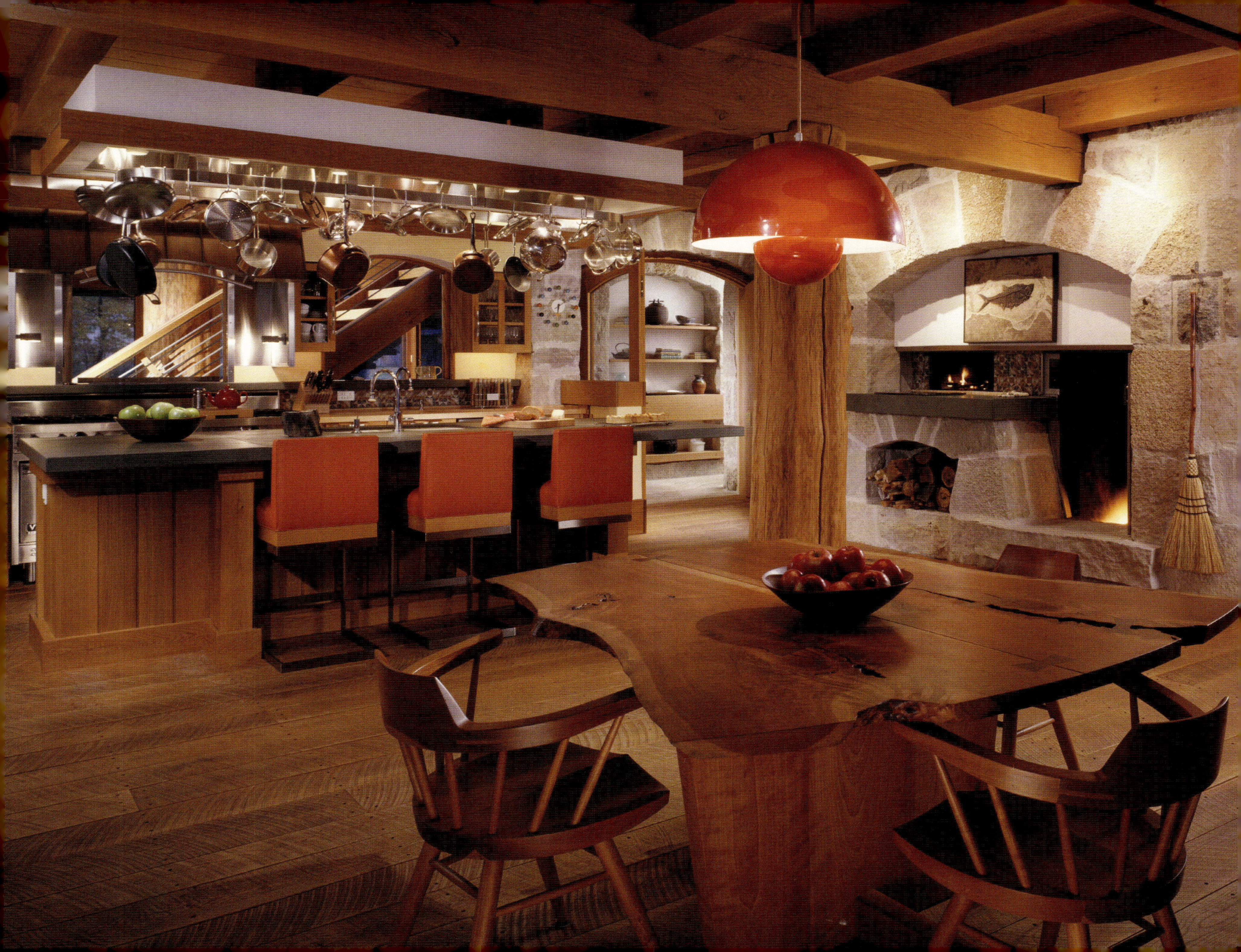

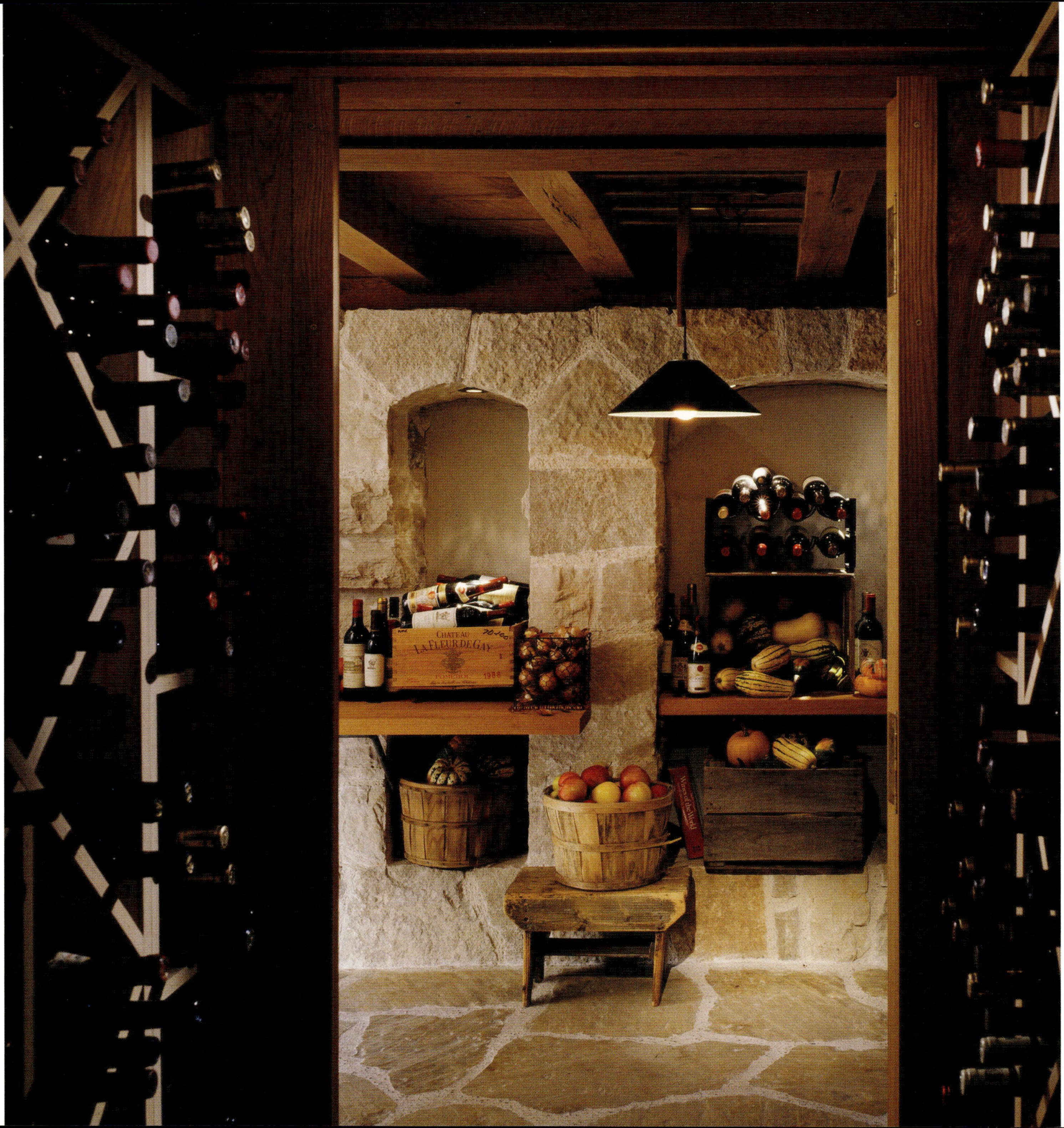
CHATEAU
LA FLEUR DE GAY
1988

May every house possess these virtues of a hut.

The primitive belongs to rich and poor alike.

Its plain, undecorated face, expressive forms,

and modesty reveal imperishable truths

and goodness resident inside its simple self.

Humility bestows this queen a gentle grace.

45

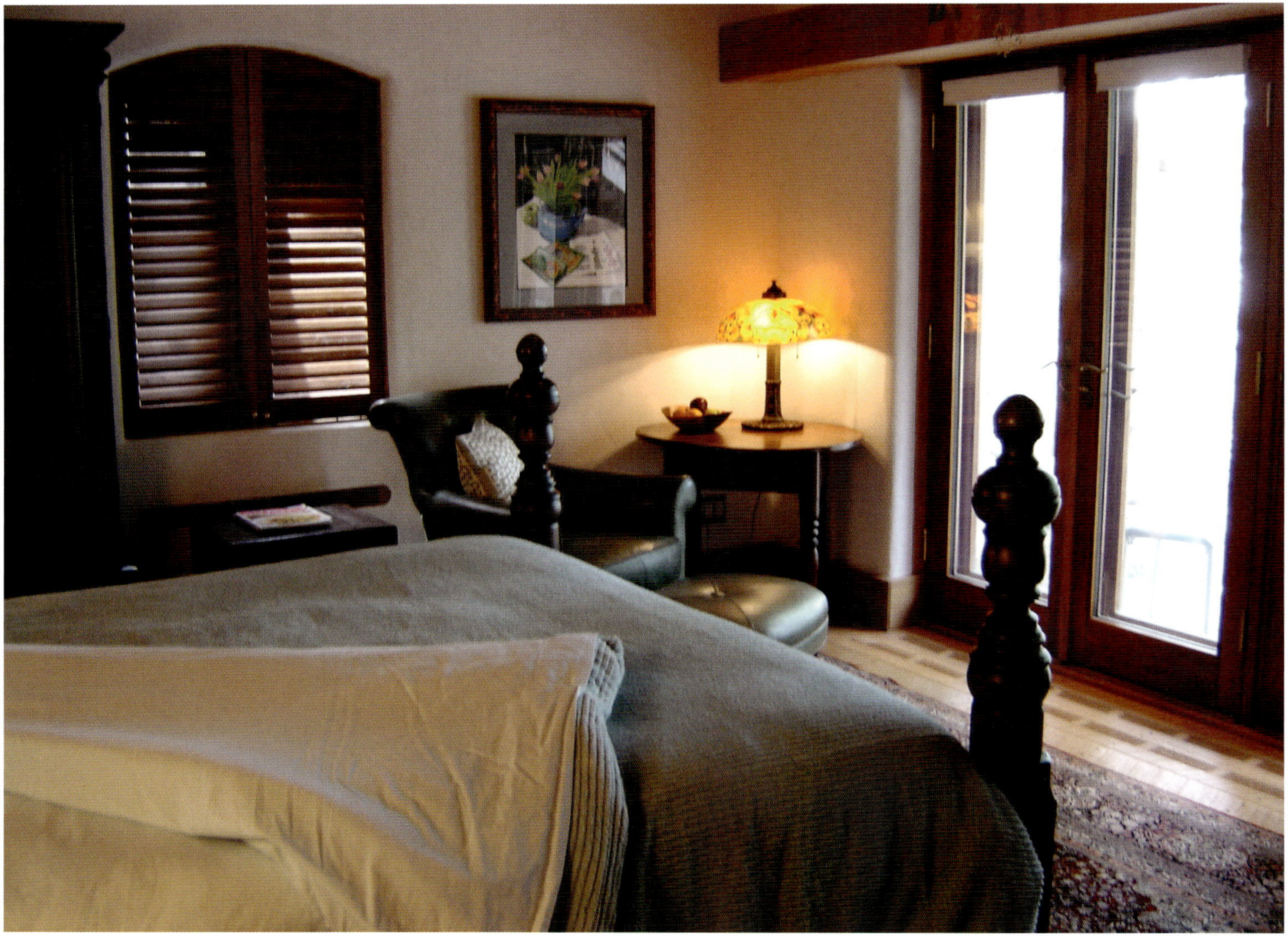

JOURNEY

Within the secret chambers of the house, we light

the flame we carry with us to humanity,

then find the rock on which to stand to orient

ourselves within opposing forces of our peers,

49

and only then, we may unite the outer world.

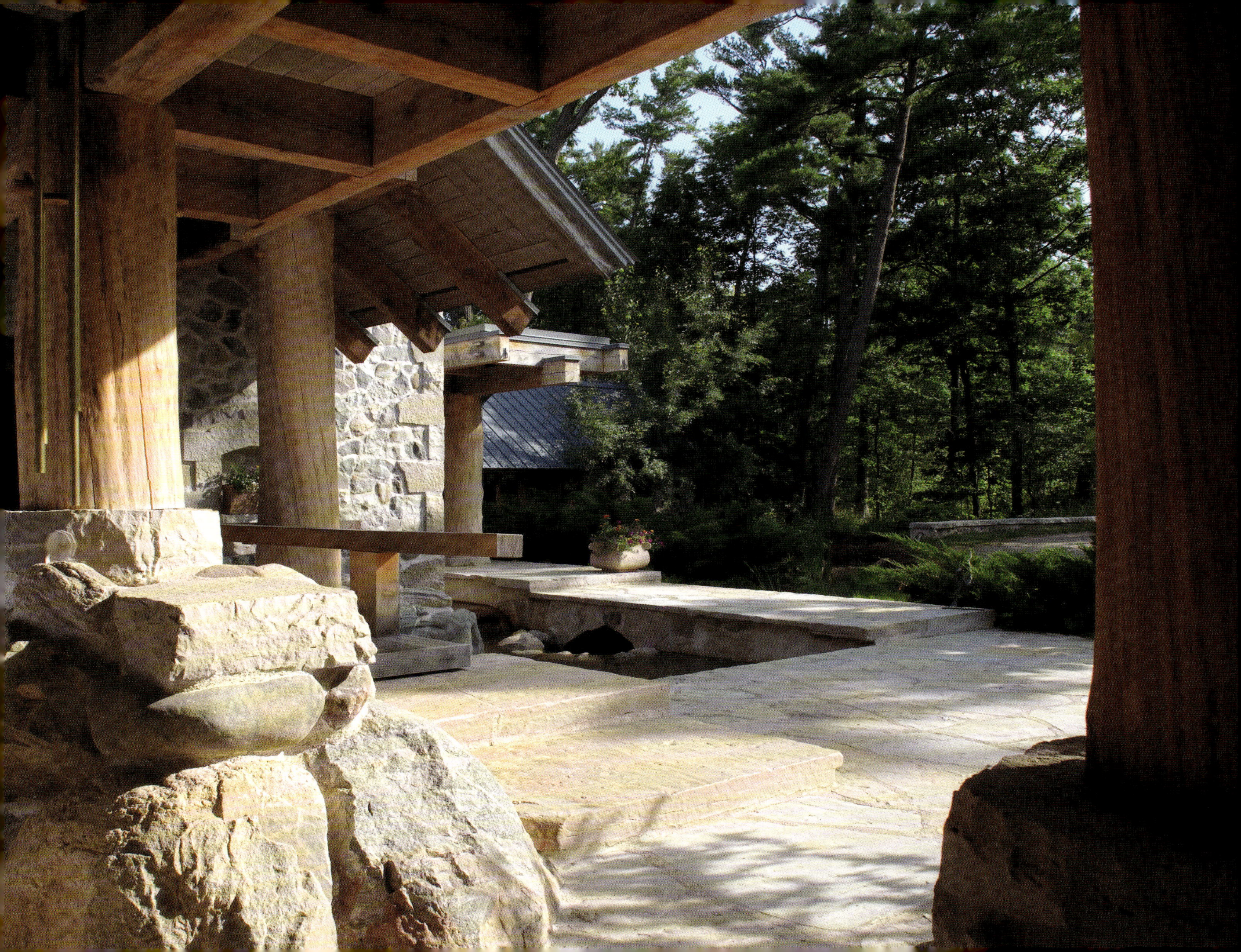

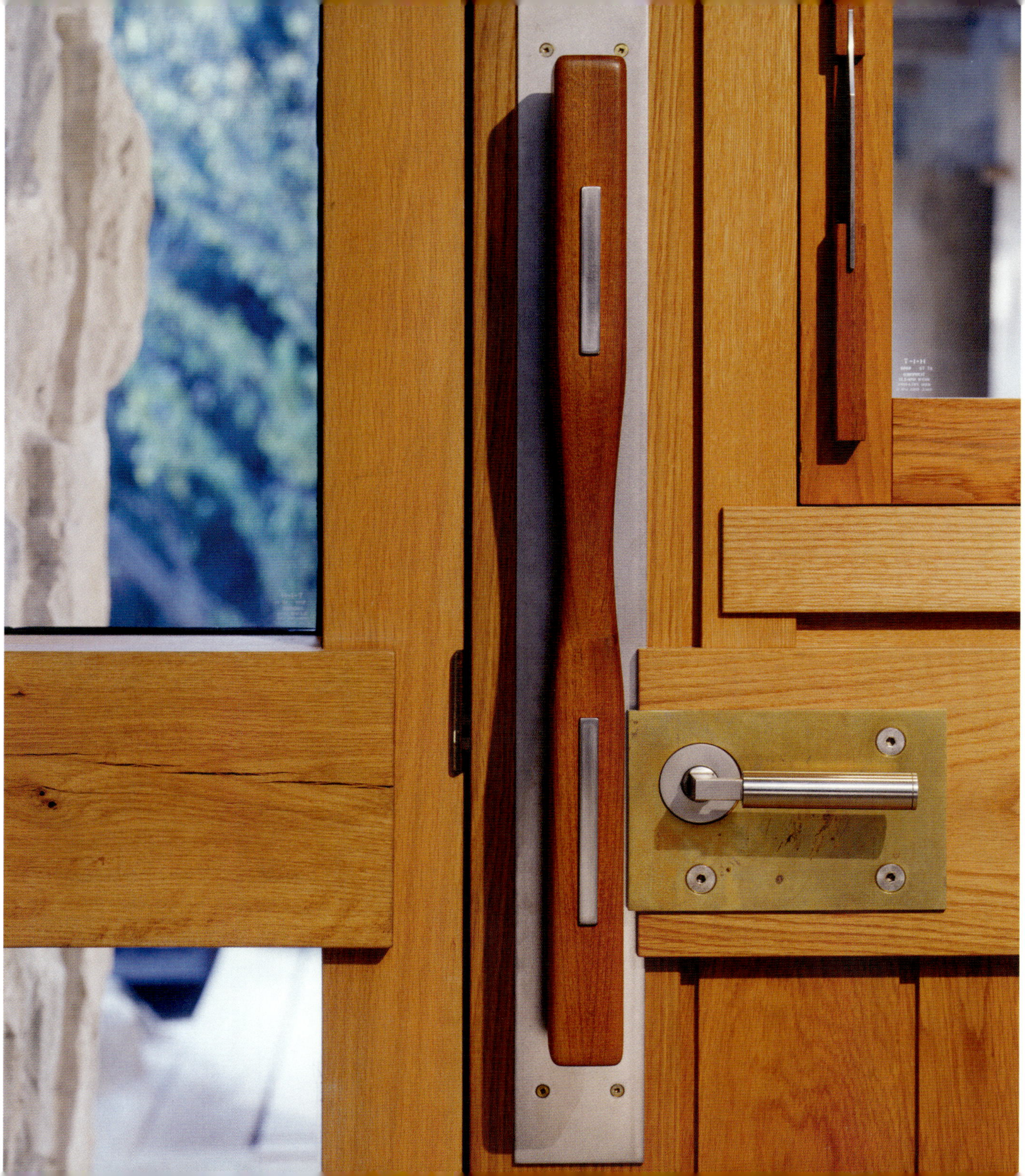

What is a door but a threshold of mystery

to close against the storms or open to the wind—

to bar the dragonflies of maps and compass box

that land within the rucksack of the youthful mind,

or open to the pilgrim seeking sanctuary?

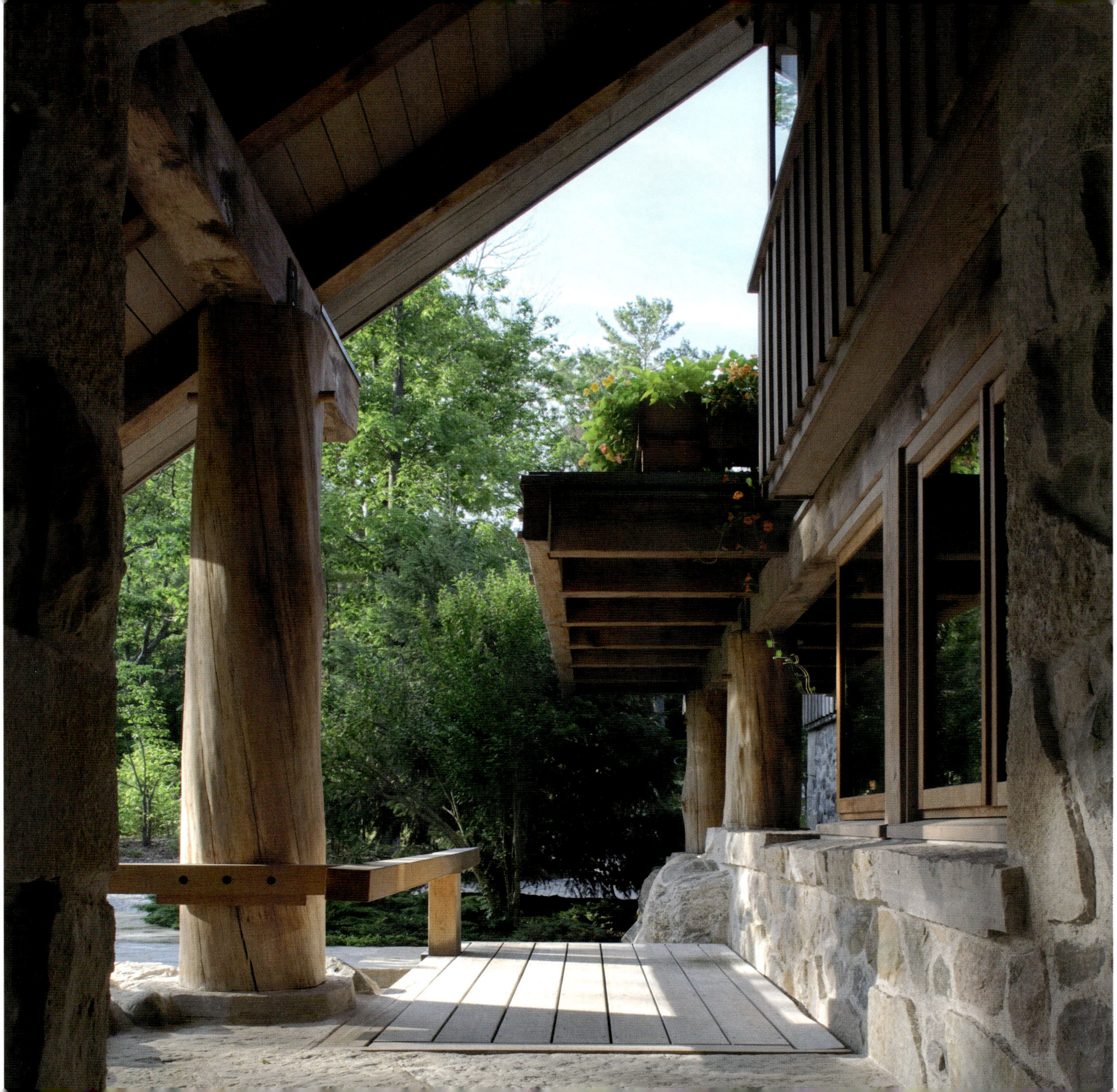

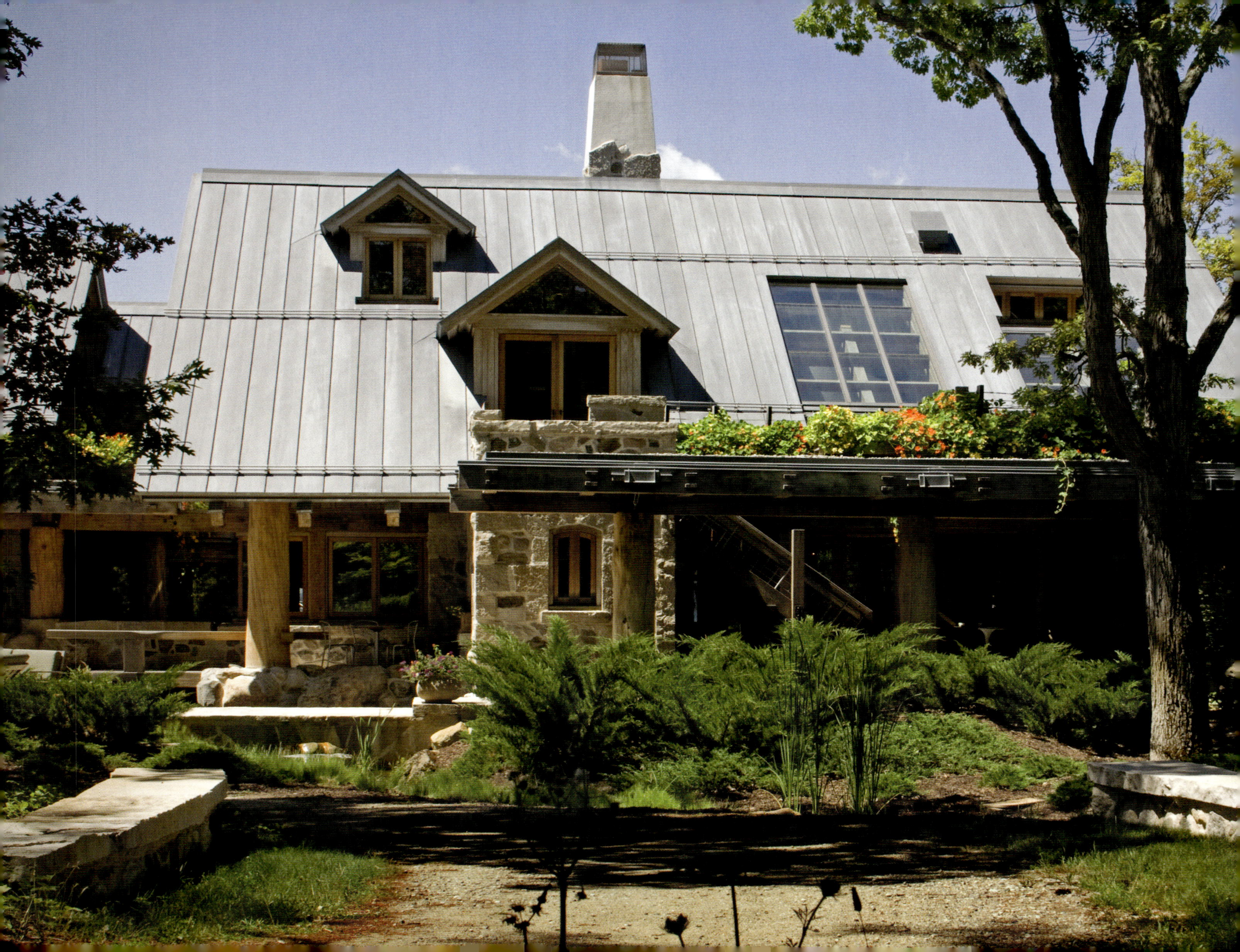

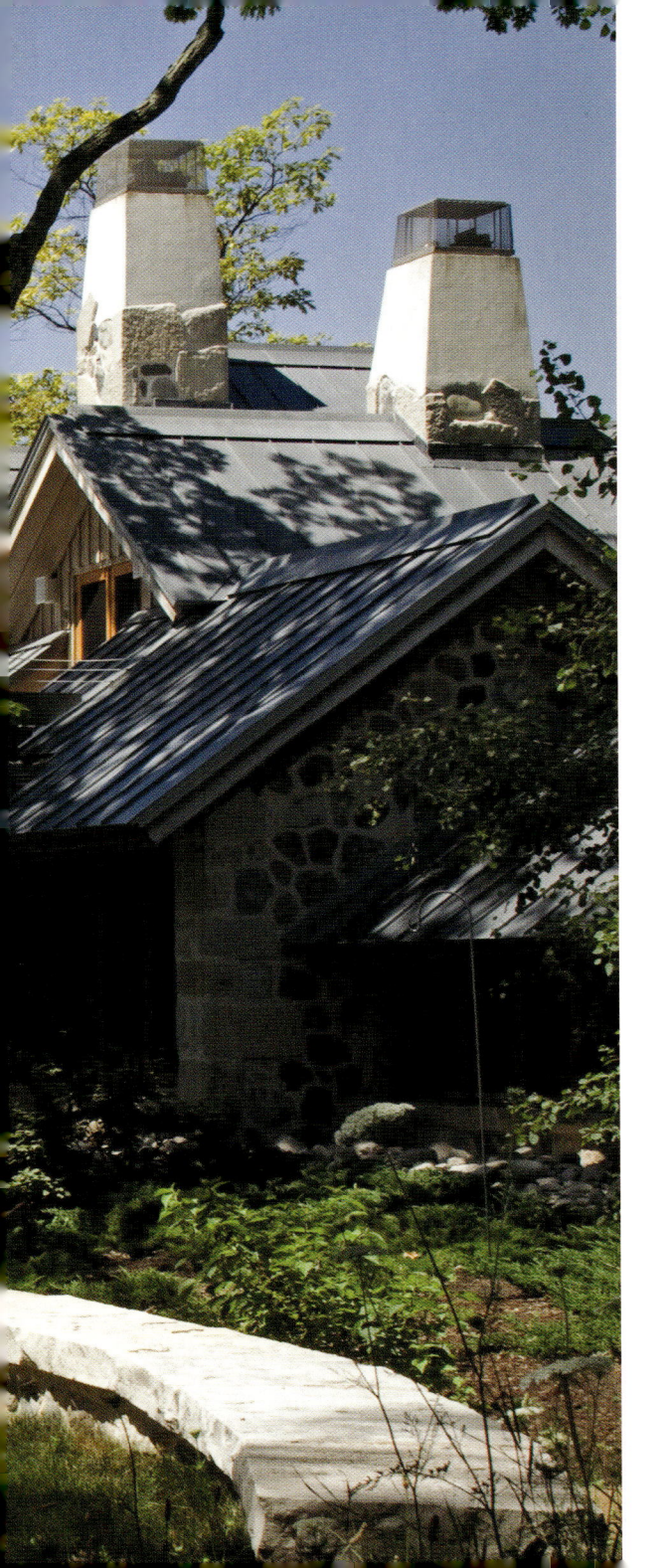

The gravel road or grassy path we choose

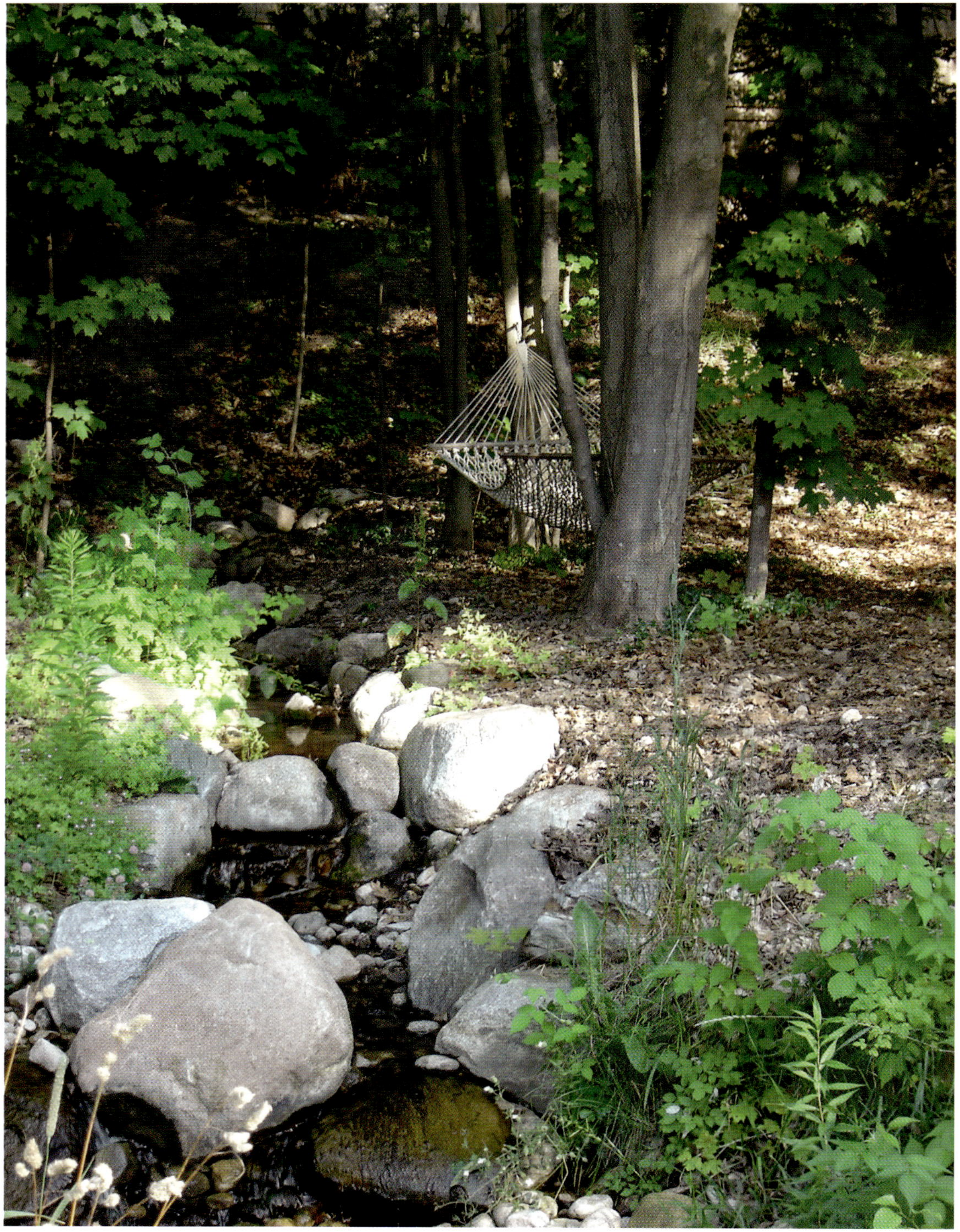

gives pace, variety and direction to our journey,

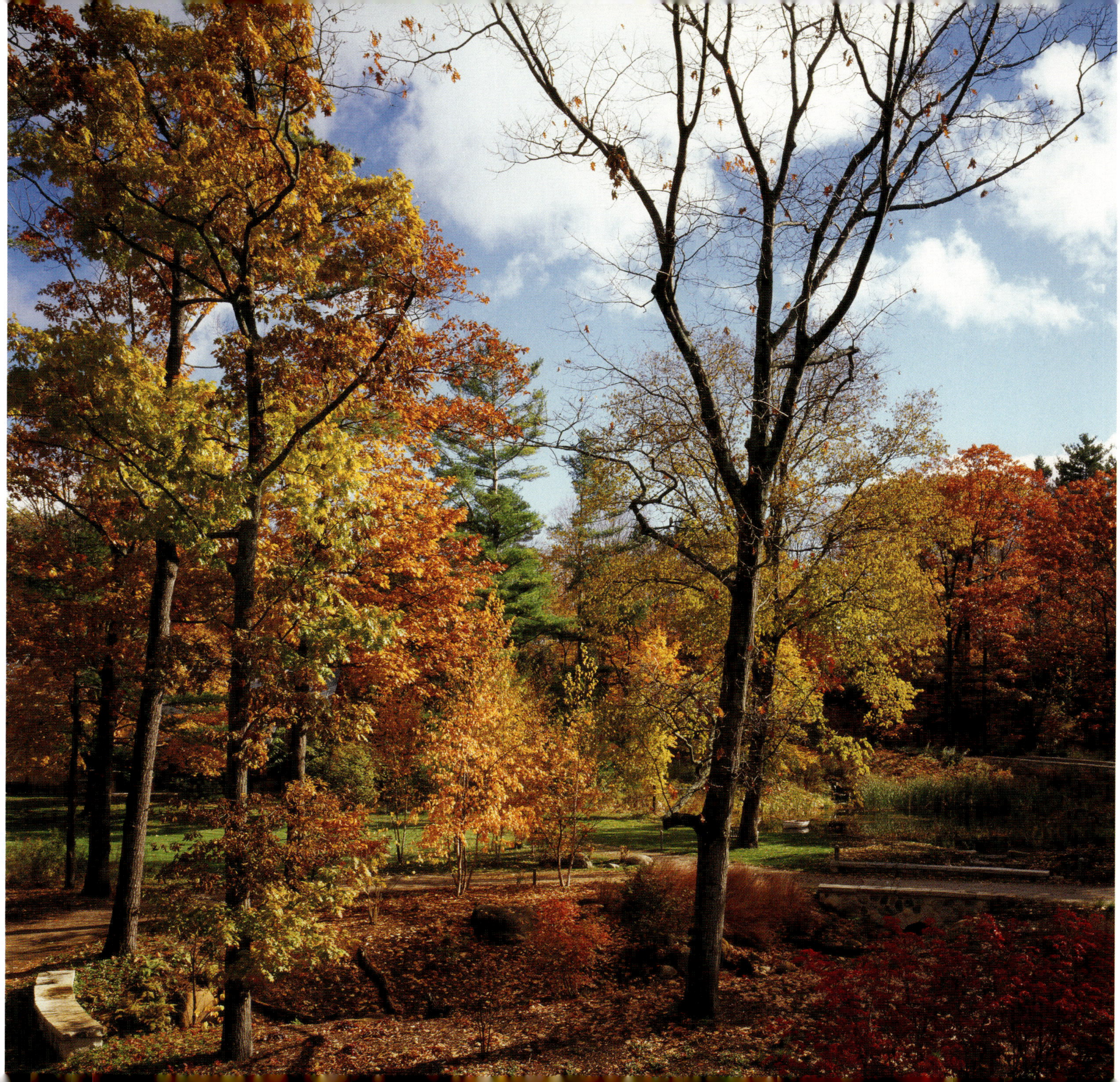

as the tree-side bench, lost valley and green meadow

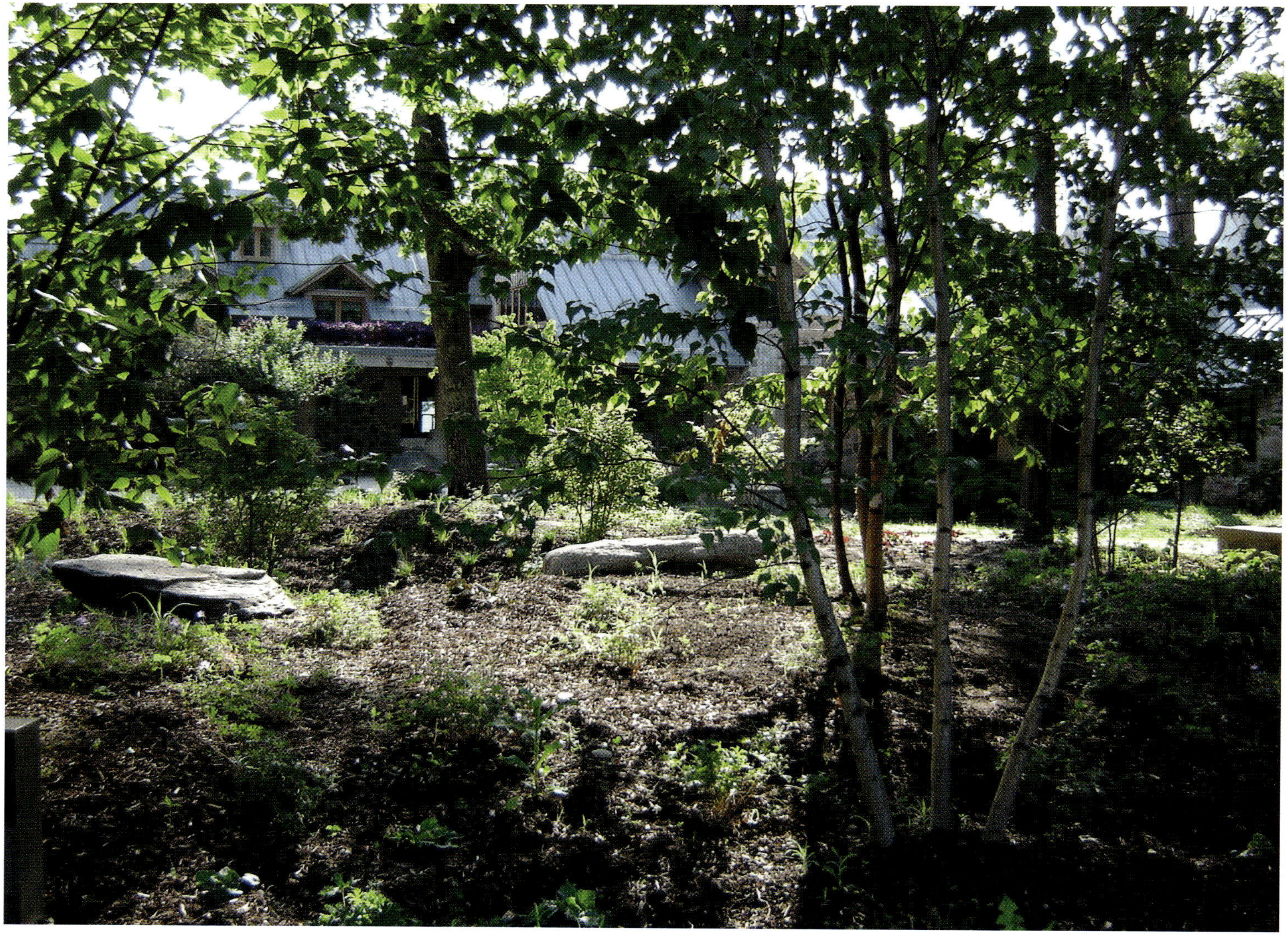

give the wild spaces and shadows of reverie

a momentary rest on the migration home.

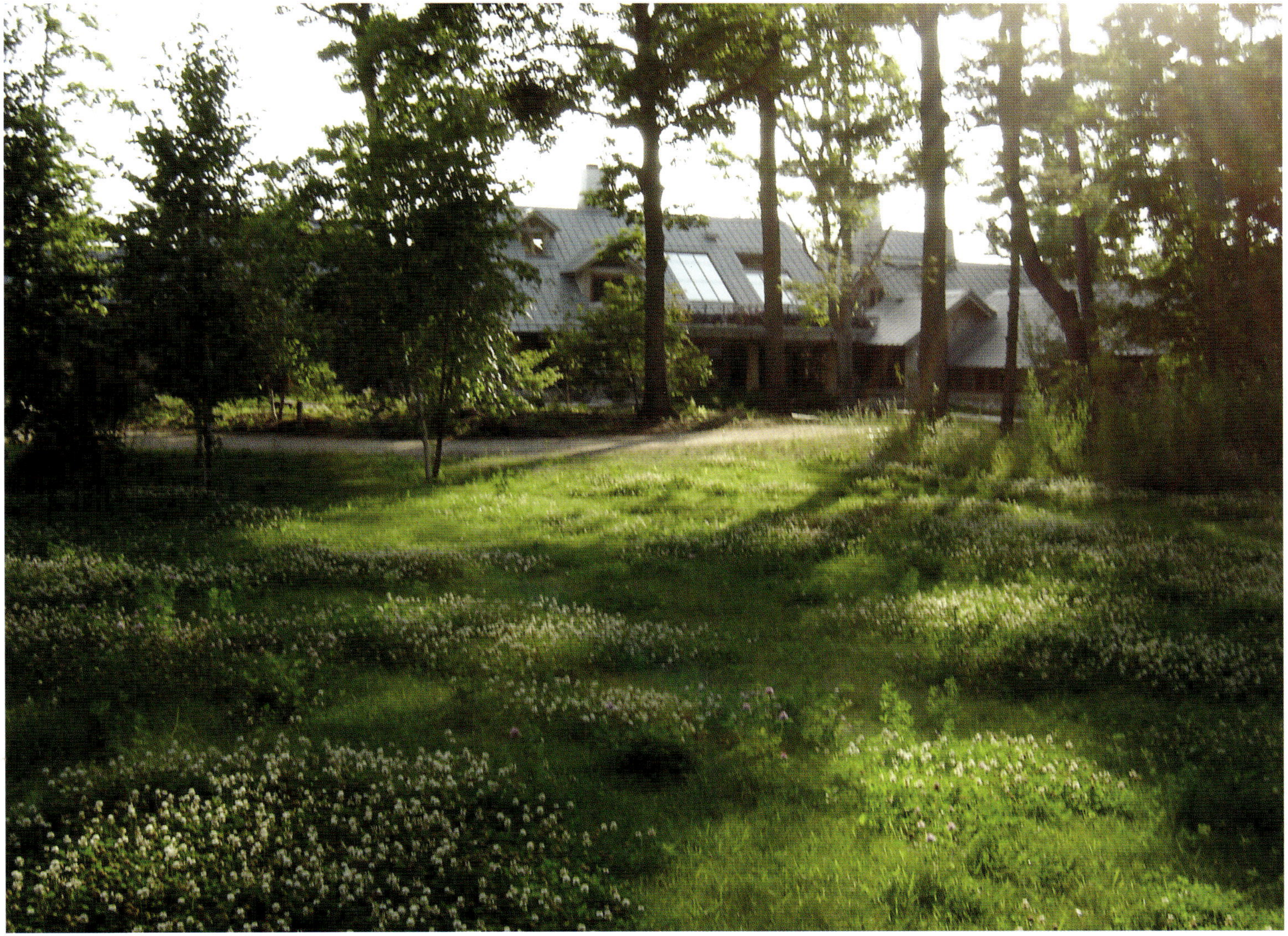

photo ©KenScottPhotography.com

We recreate the offspring of our hearts and minds,

see for ourselves the boundaries of wilderness,

explore the edges of immensity in skies

so dark that sacks of billowing starlight unfurl

to spill them out across an undulating lake.

photo ©KenScottPhotography.com

Then we go home to watch a patch of sun explore

the floor,

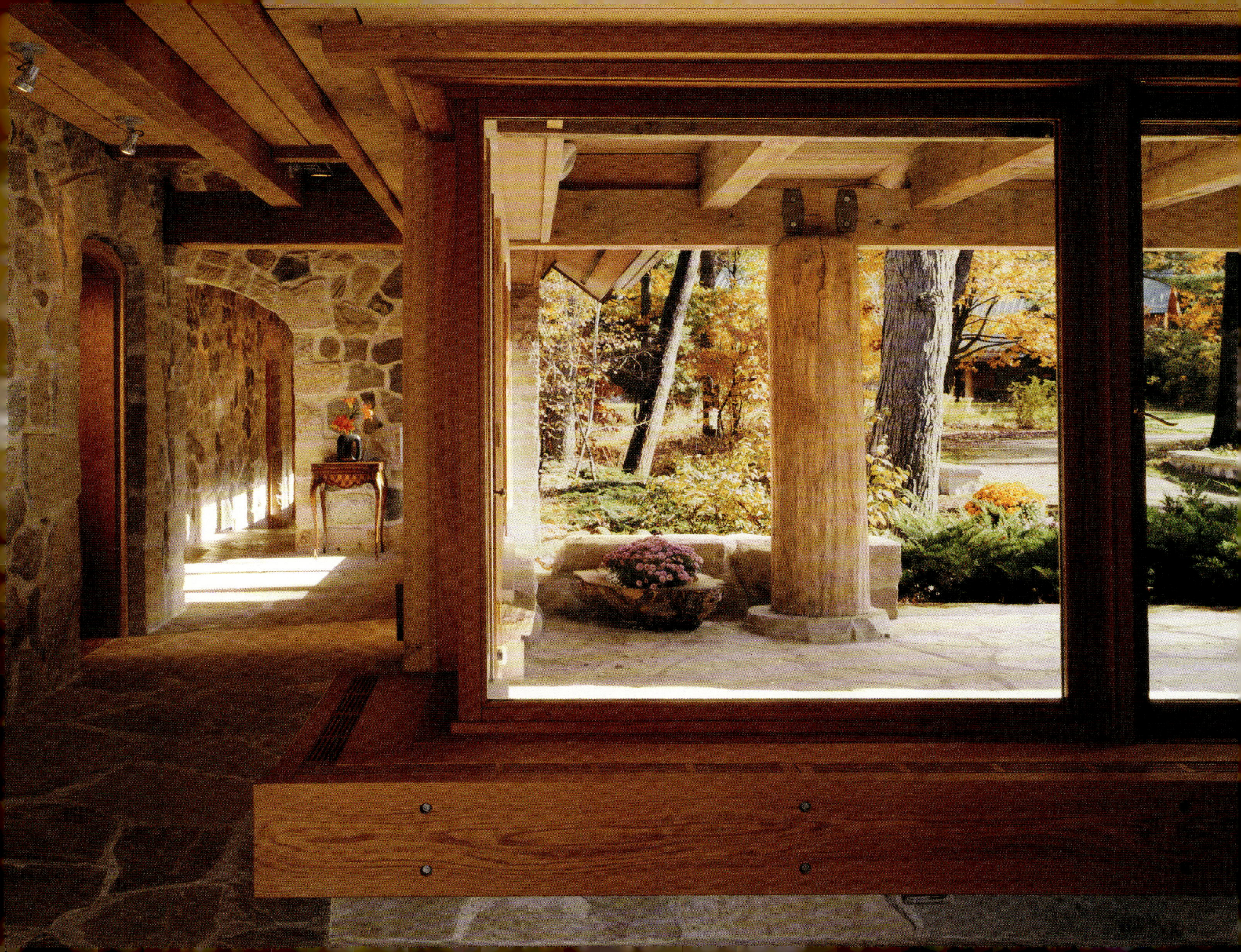

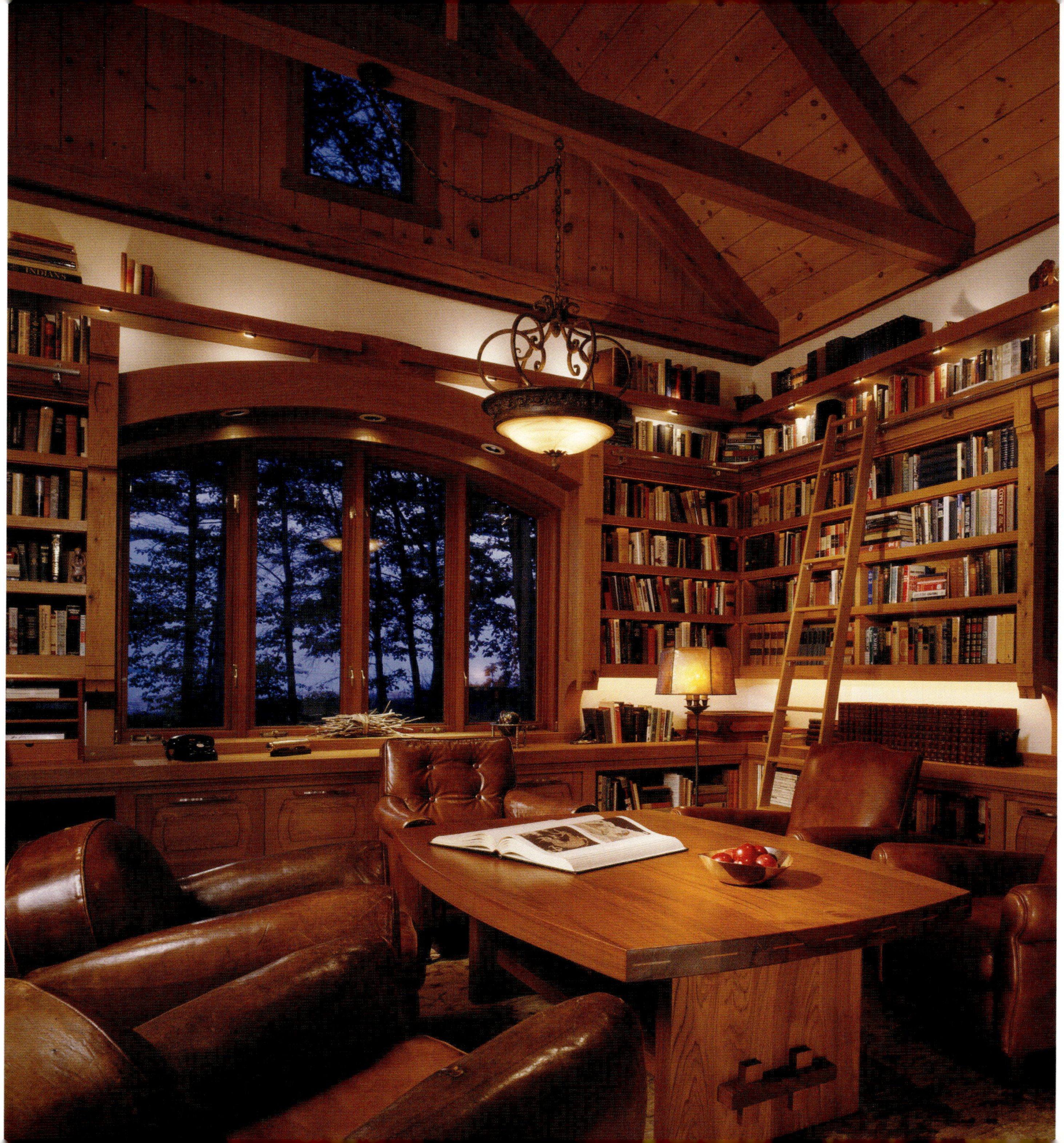

or learn to build a fortress against time

with books

and secret places of imagining,

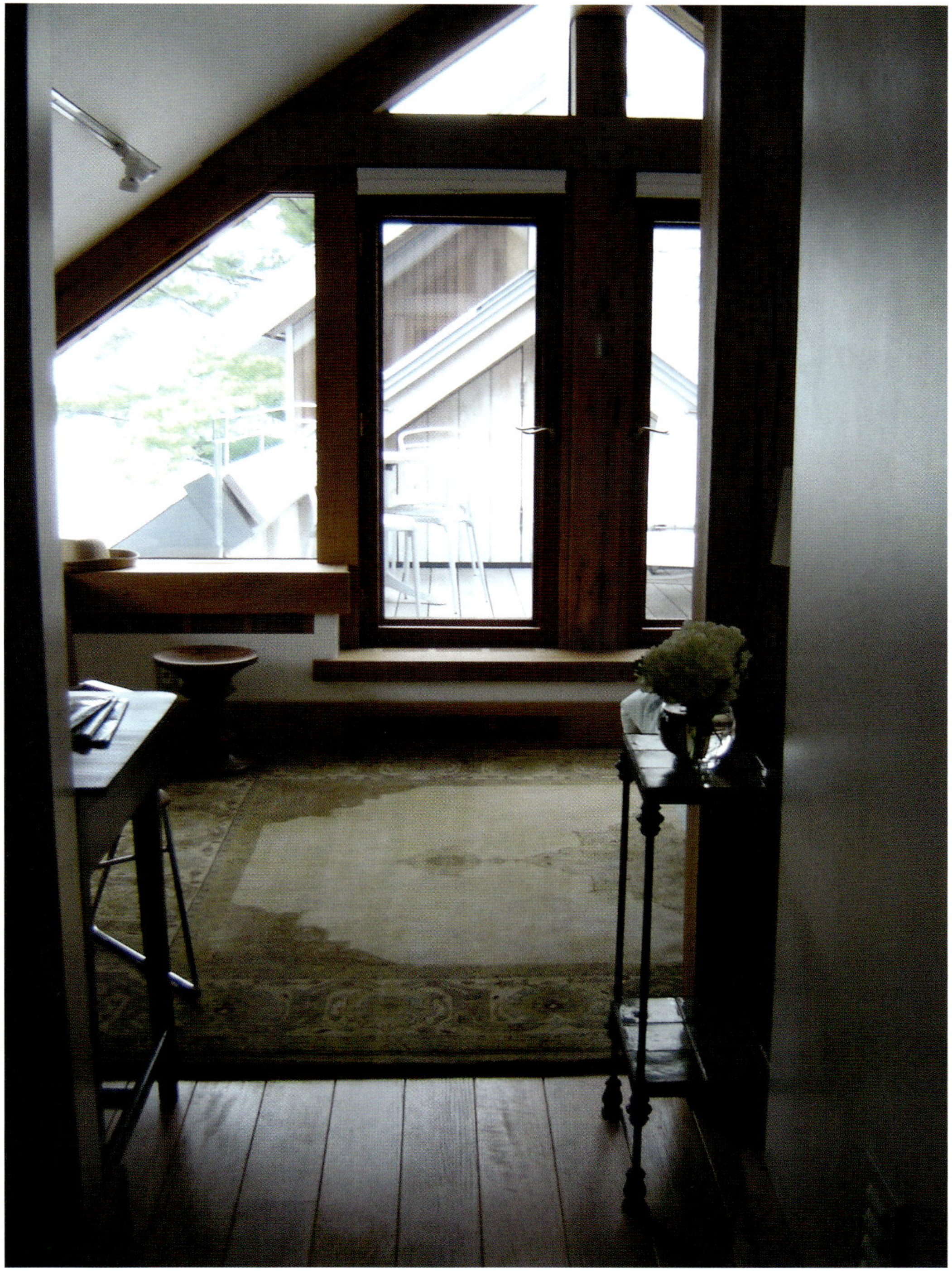

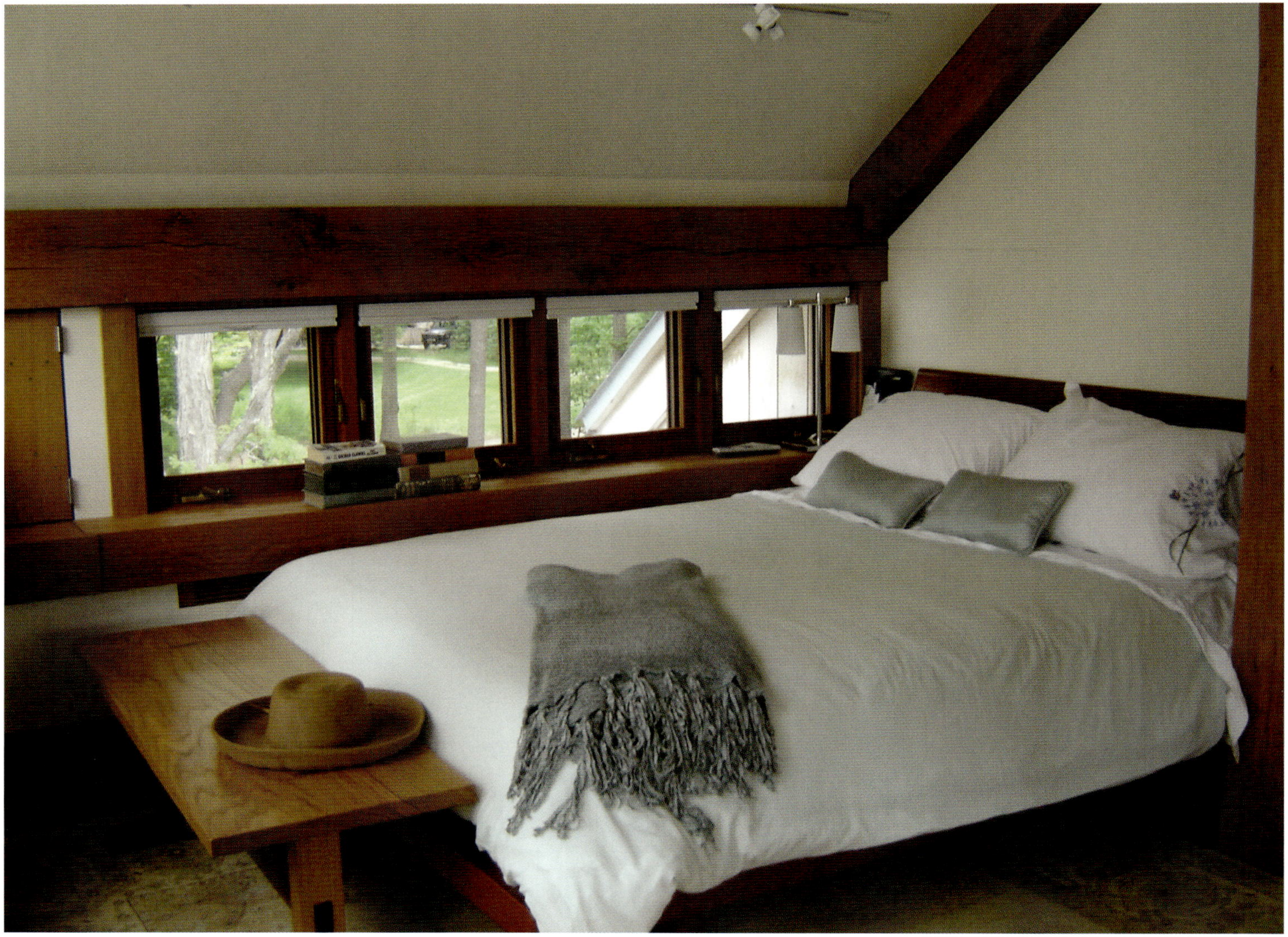

or find a way to heal in havens of retreat,

and thank our line of ancestors who brought us here.

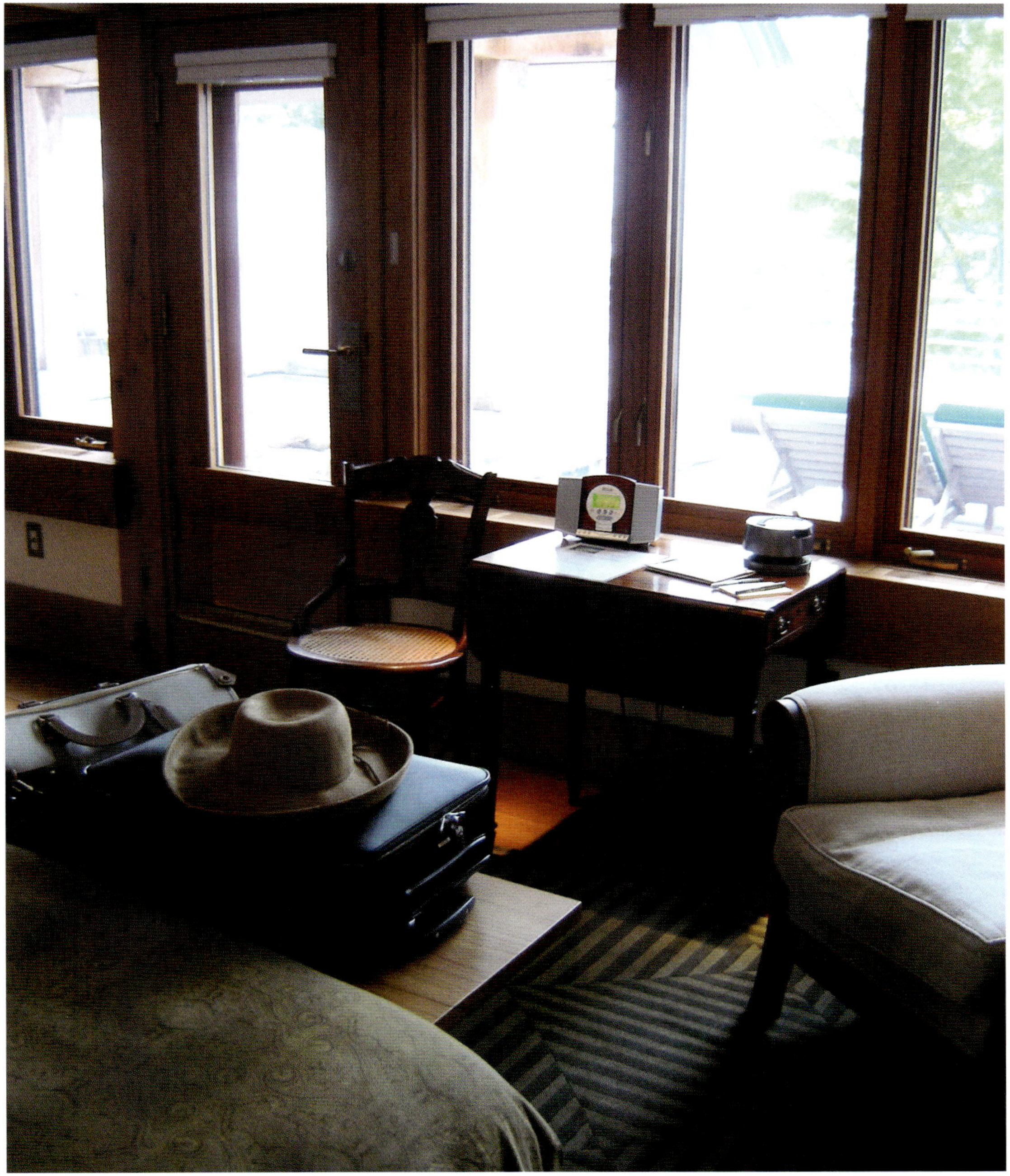

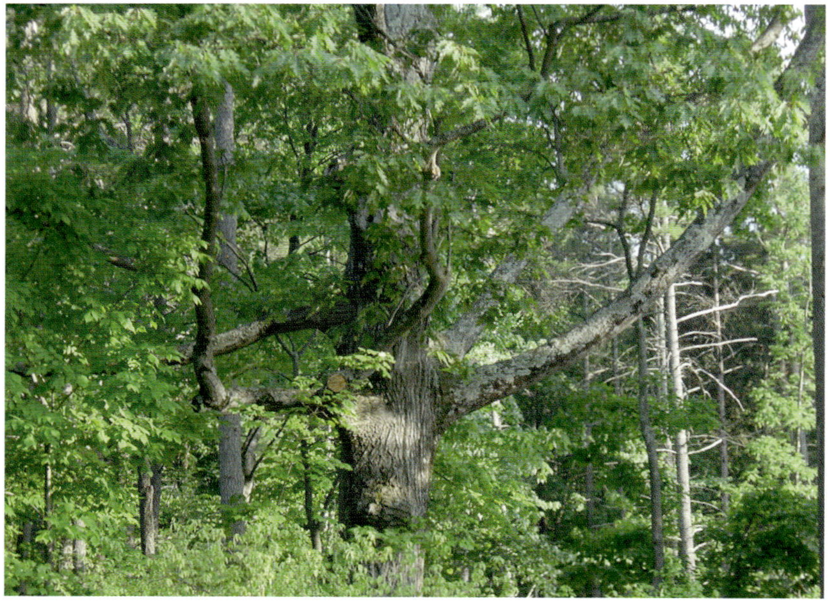

As life on Earth in all its forms first flows through plants so as we flow, a fallen leaf in gentle dew,

or swiftly down the stream, or trapped against the rocks,

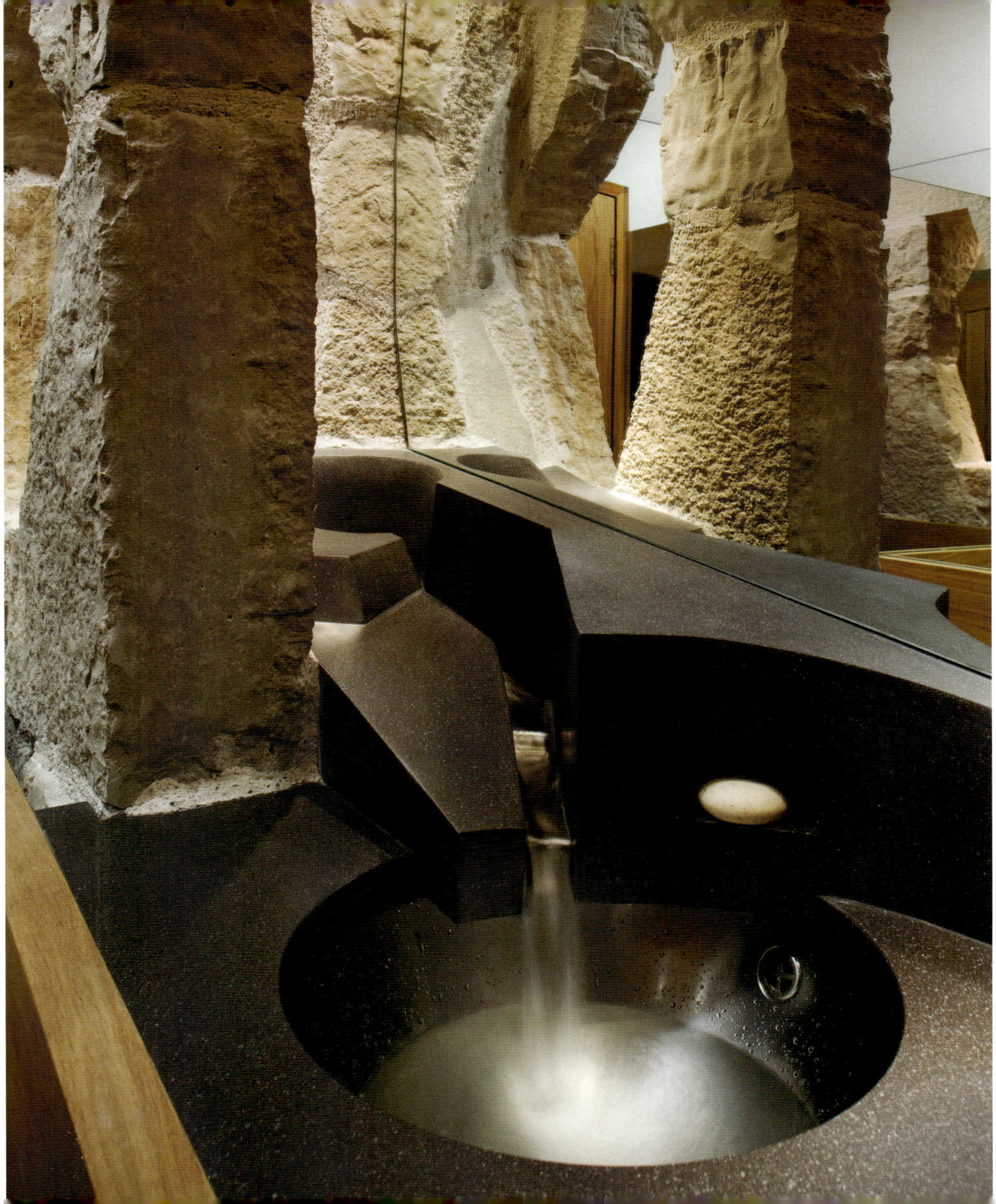

and as the water seeks the sea, we hope to find

cerulean peace and oneness in the silent deep.

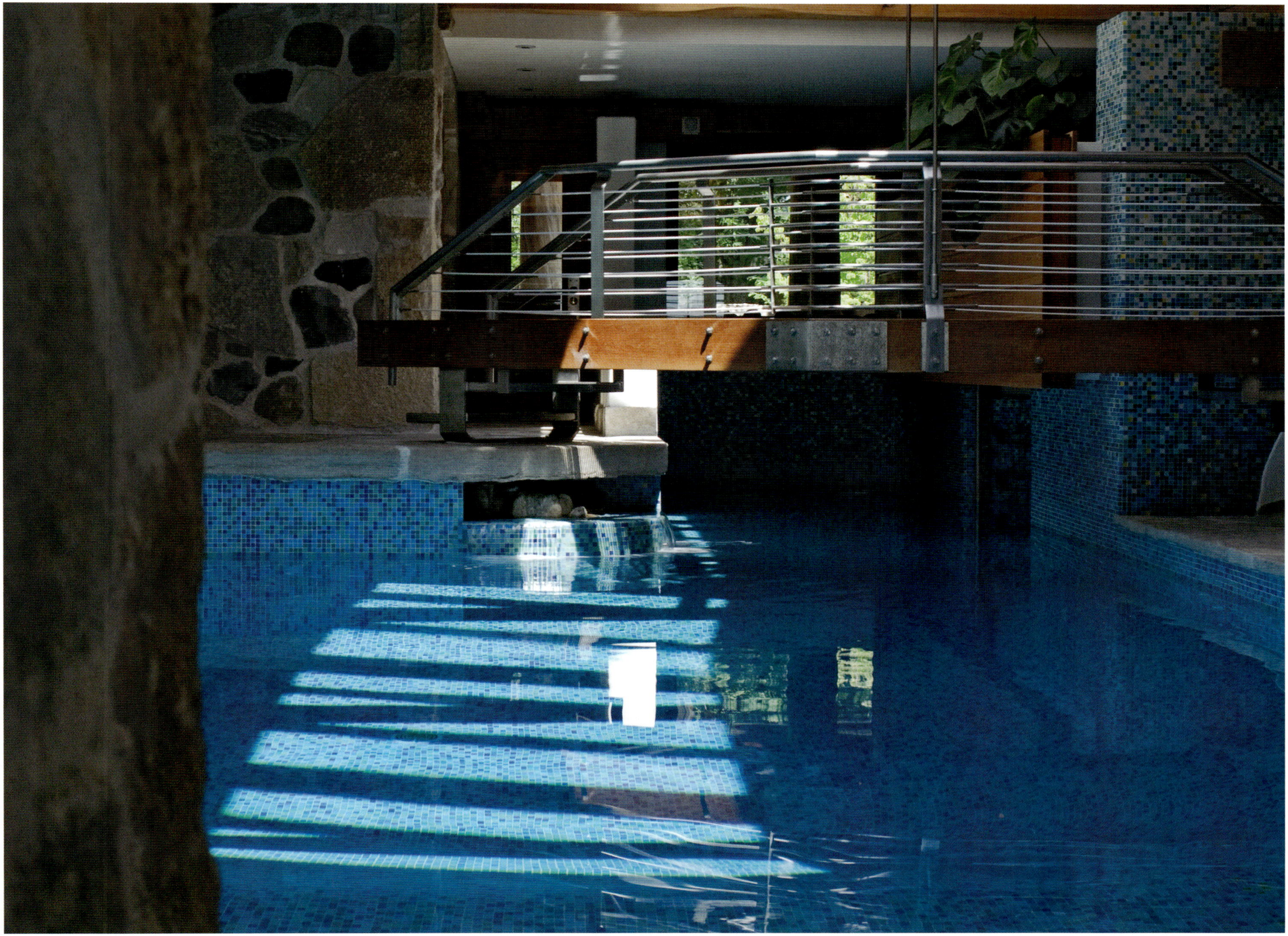

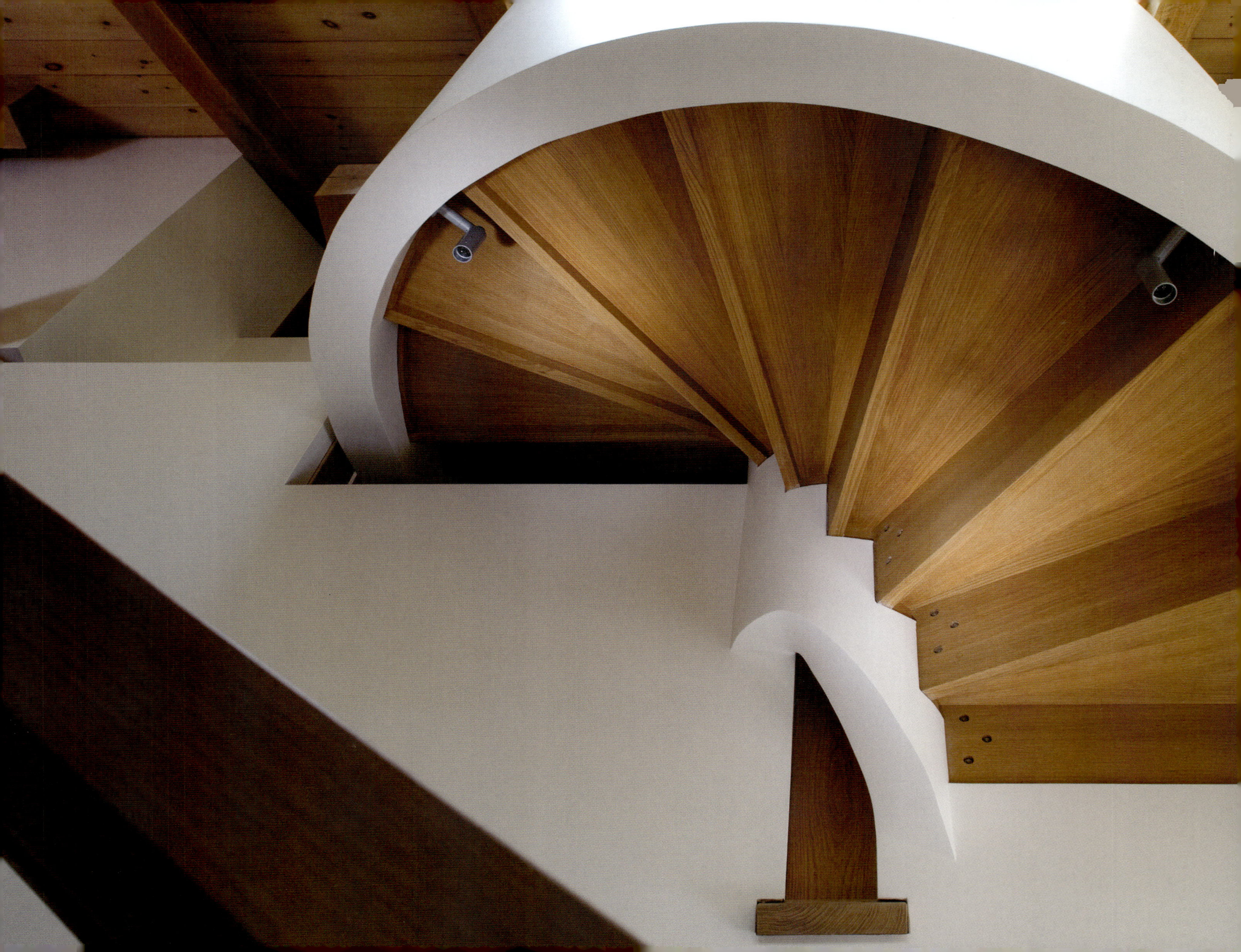

ENDURING BEAUTY

When sculpted down to its essential frame, it lives;

has strength without brutality; awareness yet,

has innocence.

88

Enduring spirits of this house

will last millennia,

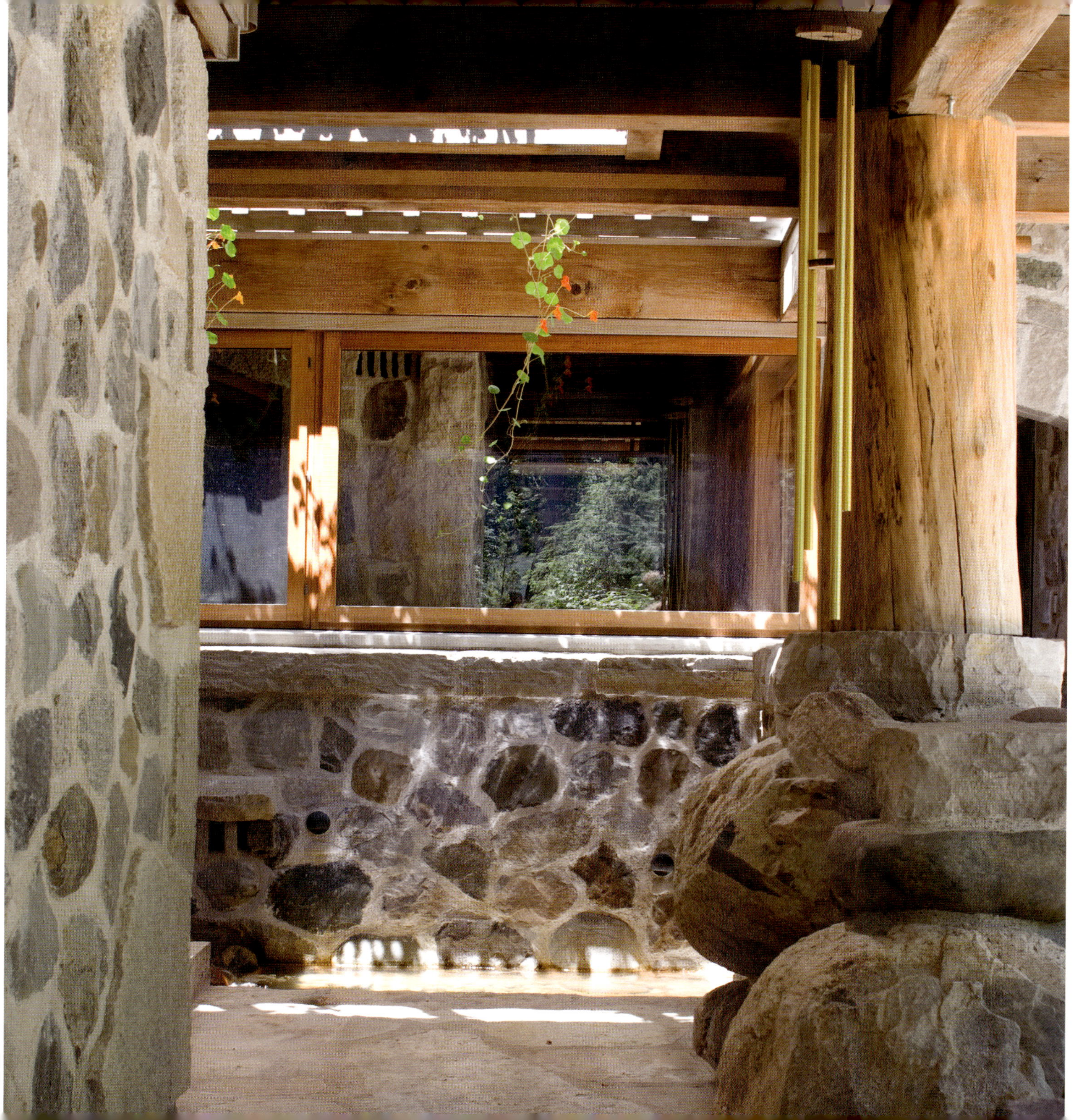

austere and worn with time,

bereft of ornament and elegant as chimes.

The house will never be more beautiful than when

great age records the stories of experience

upon the surface of its skin, or younger seem

when gratitude for life the way it is shines with

transcendent light within the windows of its soul.

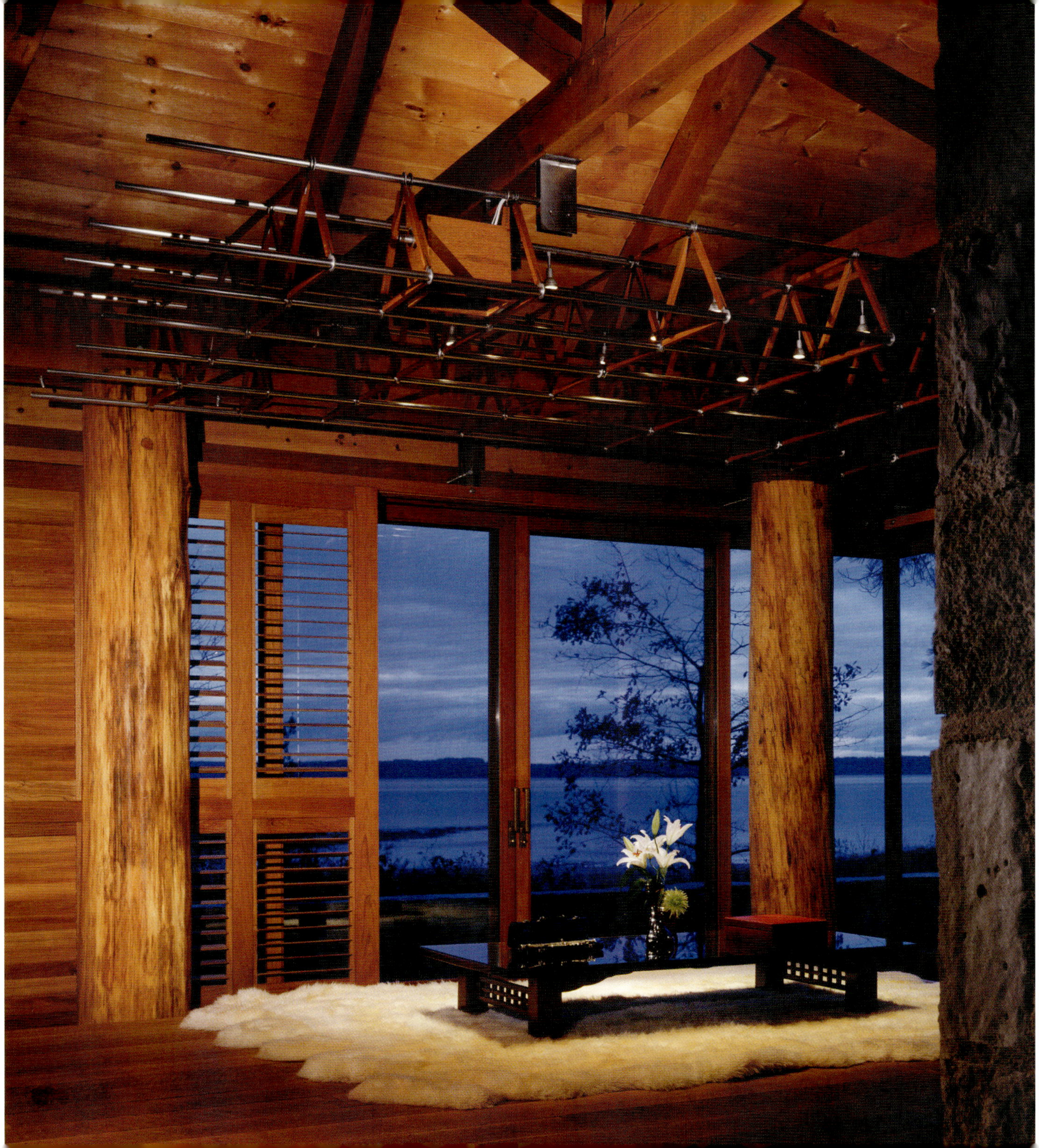

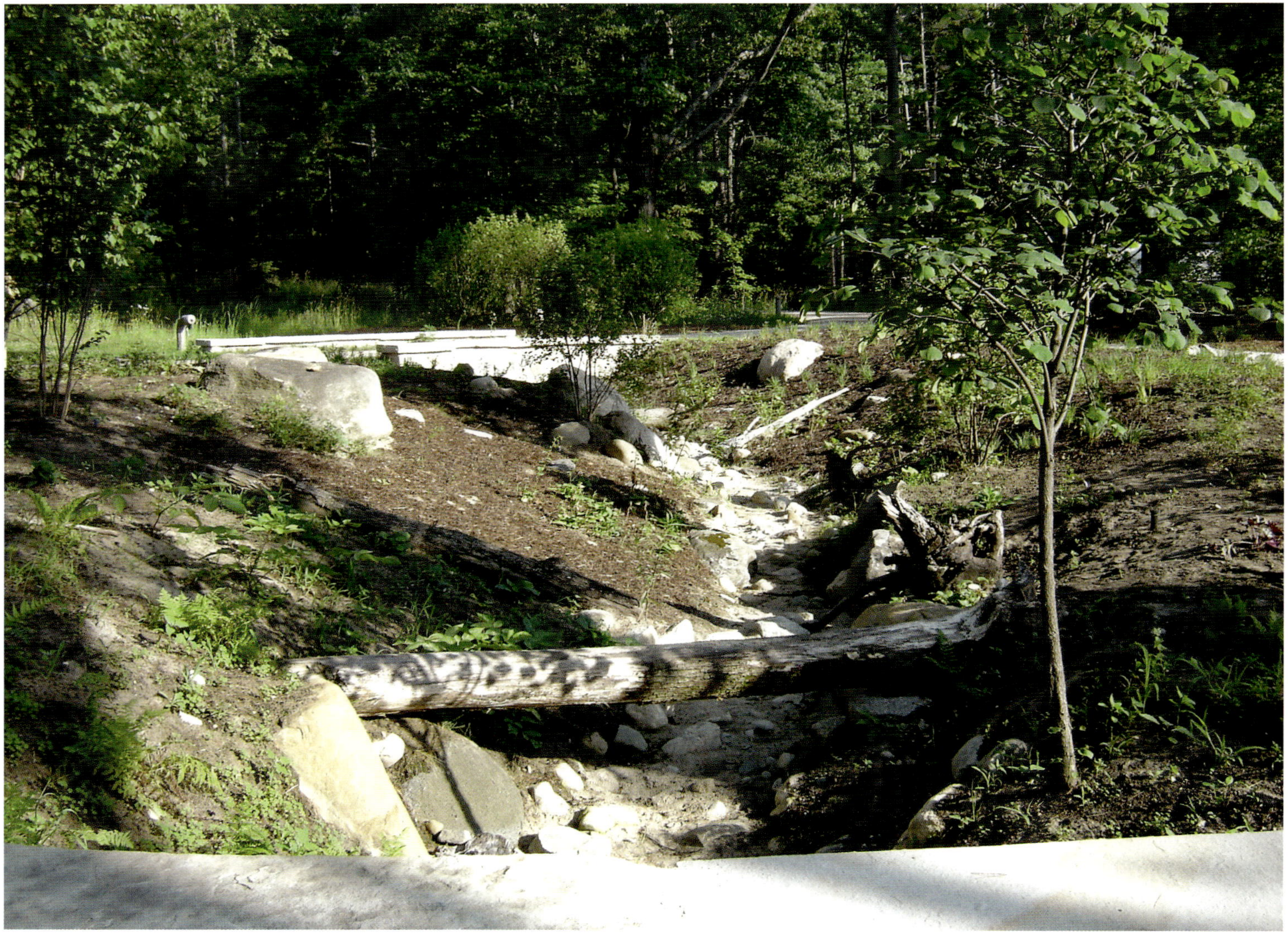

The time may come to let it go to Mother Earth.

If this should pass, where once were walls, I'll rest amid

the stones, without a roof, the rain will fall soft on

my face,

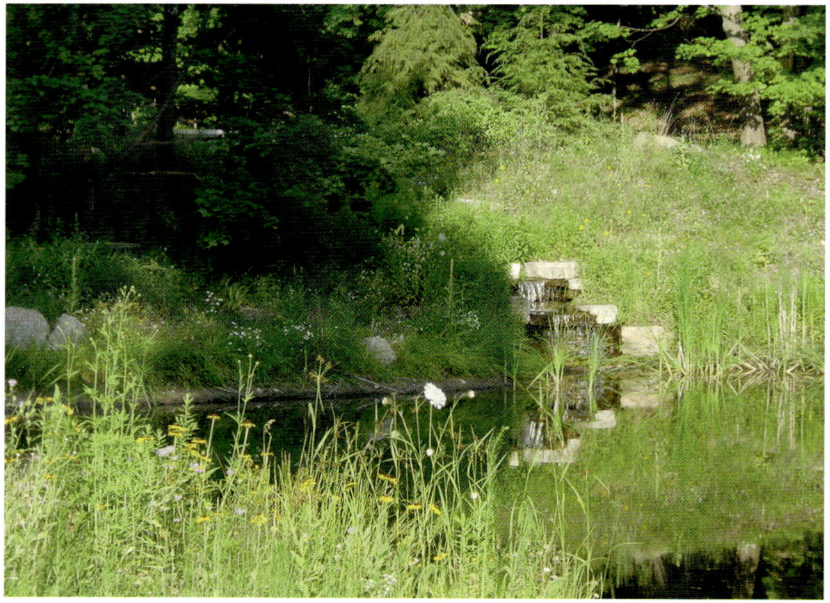

the wind, where windows were, will freely breathe

the sweetgrass scented air, and memories will live.

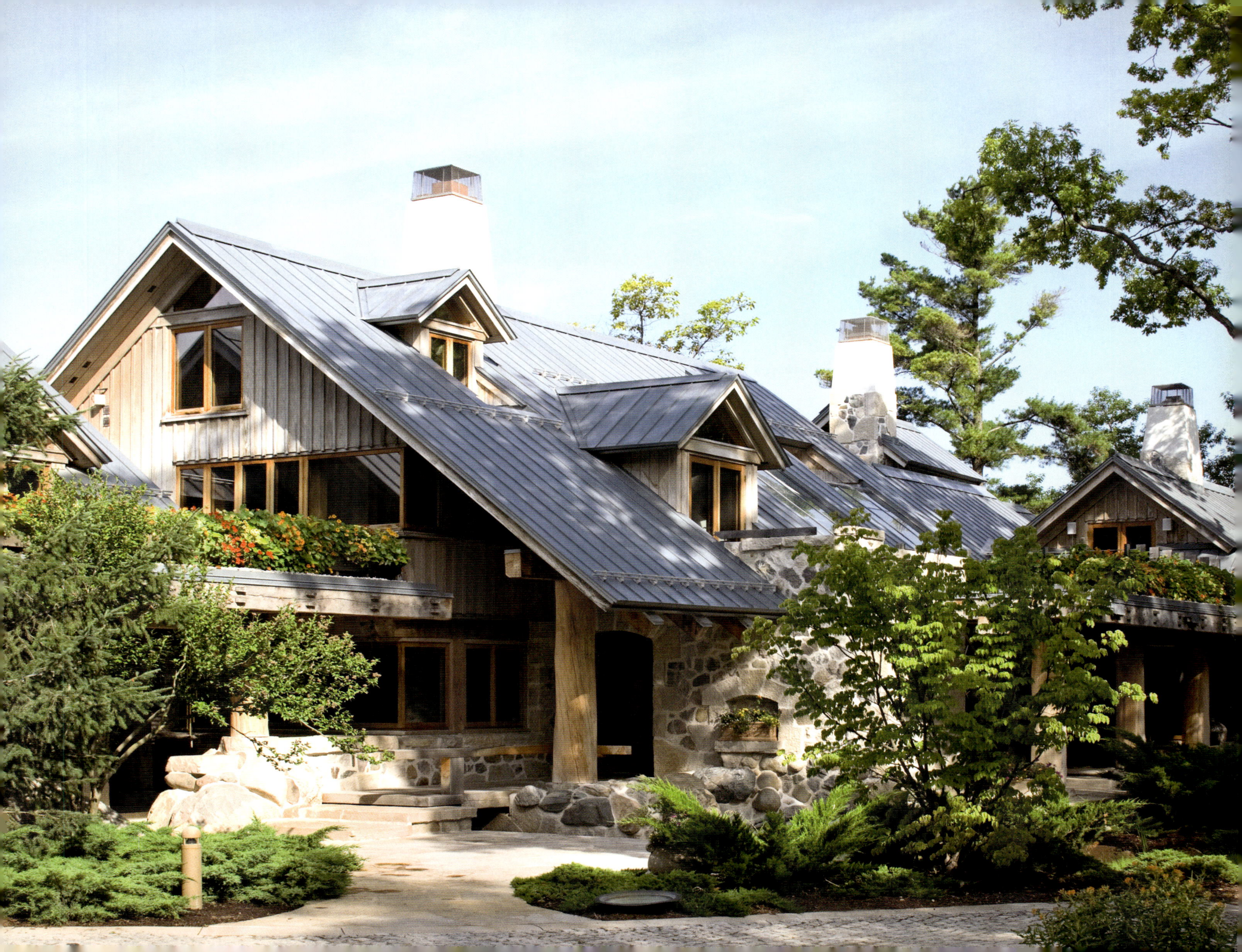

The moments perish as I write, yet still I wish

these salted stones and amber wood, in service to

the heart of goodness, last a thousand years for those

who stay and strive to make the world a better place;

or should we fail, these words inspire another hope.

SACRED SPACE
BY LESLIE LEE

PLACE

My memories are home in humble silence here

as scents of sea arise from limestone walls on days

of rain like this. I still can smell crustaceous salt

and pause in reverie as images of life

remind me of ancestral versions of myself.

I saw an ancient line of mountains in the North

arise from molten pools inside an airless world,

and seams of copper cool in Canada's granite,

and algae bloom a billion years of oxygen

into the toxic soup of atmosphere on Earth.

Tectonic forces shifted surface crusts from one

or other latitude while greenery exhaled

enriching air for tiny creatures living there,

and larger ones that fed off reefs of coral beds

in equatorial oceans that flowed offshore.

Impenetrable ice, ten thousand years ago,

a mile above the lake it left in its retreat,

inscribed a polished passage on the former bed

of ocean life still etched upon this stony floor,

and deeper still, carved lakes that filled with glacial melt.

The mammoths grazed on tundra grass before the trees

took root, and people followed with their fire and tools

by coast into the russet warmth of setting suns.

Here, eras of geology sit side by side—

ephemeral edges where the human dreams begin.

An ancient soul united with this sacred place

beneath the stars, inside the wind, within the lake.

The voices of my childhood songs and stories form

the fundamental chord of this bequeathed refrain

with harmonies to echo on a thousand years.

STRUCTURE

A white oak tree beside the creek, roots deep in soil,

then pillars up, with mirrored branches arching out

to bind the shadows of the Earth to heaven's sun.

It lives along a row of comrades cut for life,

their spirits born anew by human will to build.

The strength of oak, longevity of teak, cast brass

and hardened steel transformed by hand to timber frame.

The rocks, once strewn in fields, now tightly packed, uphold

the rolled and folded zinc of water-shedding roof.

Here, textures raw in life shine with the craft of men.

The unity of post and beam supports the group

of smaller family members notched into the walls,

those voluntary limits that define the frame.

The boundaries, of *this I am, and that I'm not*

construct the character, diversity and form.

The structure leaps and soars from roof to walls as if

to prove it moves alone from one plane to the next,

cascading risks that skip from eaves down to the floor

in steps so small that no one could object to such

a major shift in so small a space and short a time.

It tiptoes through the ancient streets and courtyards

of an older world to peer into the heart of home—

the single room of hearth and fire, of food and drink,

of songs and tales and family safe from stormy seas.

May every house possess these virtues of a hut.

The primitive belongs to rich and poor alike.

Its plain, undecorated face, expressive forms,

and modesty reveal imperishable truths

and goodness resident inside its simple self.

Humility bestows this queen a gentle grace.

JOURNEY

Within the secret chambers of the house, we light

the flame we carry with us to humanity,

then find the rock on which to stand to orient

ourselves within opposing forces of our peers,

and only then, we may unite the outer world.

What is a door but a threshold of mystery

to close against the storms or open to the wind—

to bar the dragonflies of maps and compass box

that land within the rucksack of the youthful mind,

or open to the pilgrim seeking sanctuary?

The gravel road or grassy path we choose gives pace,

variety and direction to our journey,

as the tree-side bench, lost valley and green meadow

give the wild spaces and shadows of reverie

a momentary rest on the migration home.

We recreate the offspring of our hearts and minds,

see for ourselves the boundaries of wilderness,

explore the edges of immensity in skies

so dark that sacks of billowing starlight unfurl

to spill them out across an undulating lake.

Then we go home to watch a patch of sun explore

the floor, or learn to build a fortress against time

with books and secret places of imagining,

or find a way to heal in havens of retreat,

and thank our line of ancestors who brought us here.

As life on Earth in all its forms first flows through plants

so as we flow, a fallen leaf in gentle dew,

or swiftly down the stream, or trapped against the rocks,

and as the water seeks the sea, we hope to find

cerulean peace and oneness in the silent deep.

ENDURING BEAUTY

When sculpted down to its essential frame, it lives;

has strength without brutality; awareness yet,

has innocence. Enduring spirits of this house

will last millennia, austere and worn with time,

bereft of ornament and elegant as chimes.

The house will never be more beautiful than when

great age records the stories of experience

upon the surface of its skin, or younger seem

when gratitude for life the way it is shines with

transcendent light within the windows of its soul.

The time may come to let it go to Mother Earth.

If this should pass, where once were walls, I'll rest amid

the stones, without a roof, the rain will fall soft on

my face, the wind, where windows were, will freely breathe

the sweetgrass scented air, and memories will live.

The moments perish as I write, yet still I wish

these salted stones and amber wood, in service to

the heart of goodness, last a thousand years for those

who stay and strive to make the world a better place;

or should we fail, these words inspire another hope.

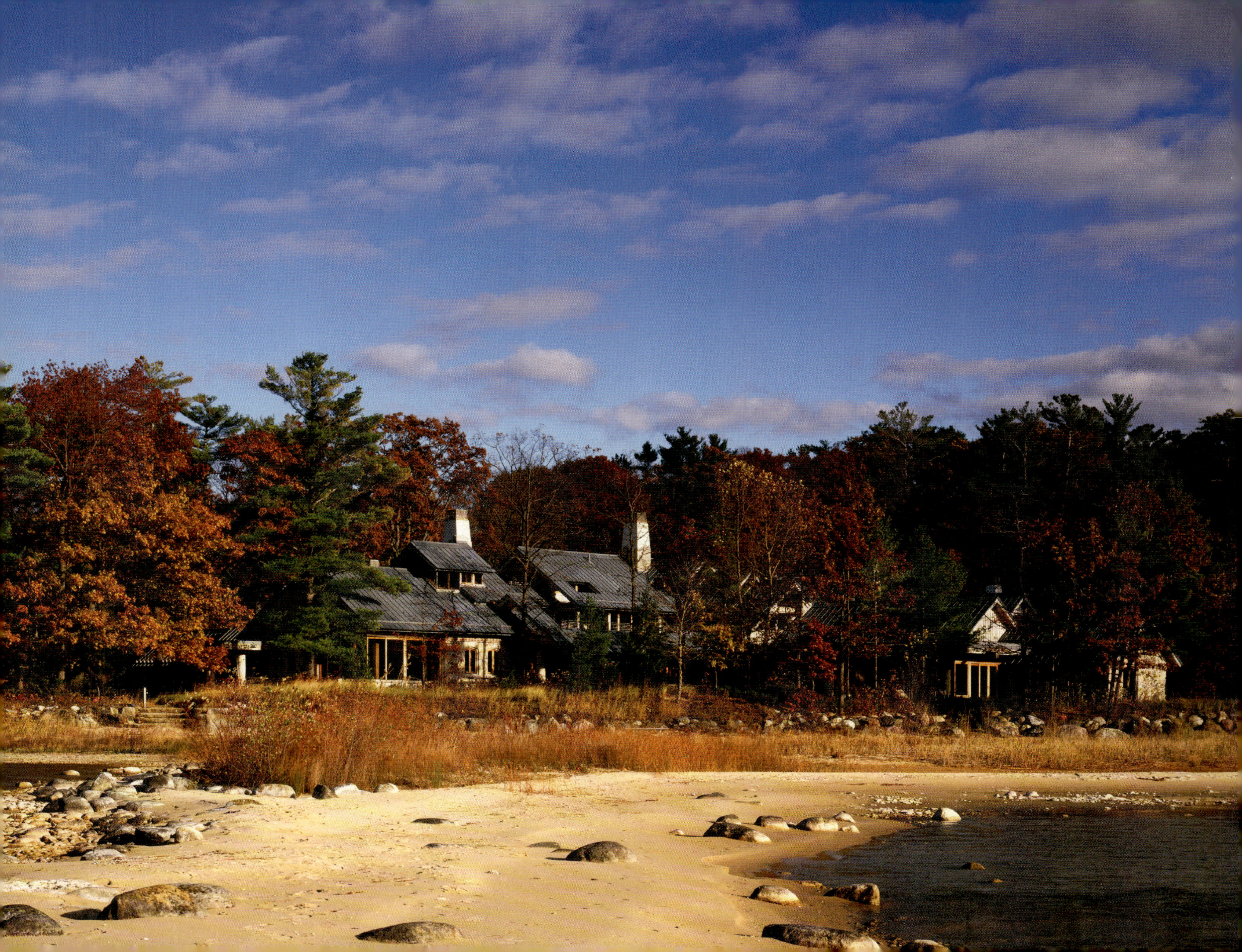

THANK YOU

Universe who made this beautiful place,
forebears who brought life down the line to me,
Pearl clan who gave me the rock to stand on,
friends who listen, care, and speak their minds,
colleagues who enable the work be done.

To architect Roger A. Hummel whose genius for design and engineering is evident in every detail of Pine Hollow, a thousand blessings. Thank you to all of the workers and craftsmen, who at the pinnacle of their craft, built the house.

Special thanks to Mary Meredith and Byrdie Butka for helping with the details of making this book a reality; to Yvonne Fetig Roehler for the beautiful layouts and Leah Nicholson for production management, both of Jenkins Group, Inc.; to the photographers at Hedrich Blessing in Chicago and Nancy Crafts of Sausalito for the gorgeous photographs of the house and grounds, and to local photographer, Ken Scott, for the extraordinary photographs of our natural home in Northwest Lower Michigan; to author Jerry Dennis whose positive feedback gave me the confidence to proceed; to Diana Beresford-Kroeger for teaching me about the importance of native plants; to Susie Galbraith, Patrick Harrington and Paul Tegel for patiently listening to early versions; to Dale Hull who has come to lead the nonprofit Pine Hollow Institute which inspired me to transform my picture album, "Pine Hollow: A Vernacular Architecture" into this real book, *Sacred Space: Pine Hollow*; to Carl Ganter, Jerry Dennis, Diana Beresford-Kroeger and Jon Miller for their kind words; and to my children for their love and encouragement.

In gratitude, Leslie Lee

PINE HOLLOW

Owner and Founder, Leslie Lee

Architect, Roger A. Hummel

Construction Manager and General Carpentry, Comstock Construction

PRINCIPAL CRAFTSMEN

Site Supervisor, Fred Marsh of Comstock Construction

Timber Frame, Robert Foulkes of TimberSmart

Electric, Windemuller Electric, Inc.

Plumbing and Heating, Arms & Cole

Library and Doors, Gary Cheadle, et al, of Woodbine

Kitchen Carpentry, Paul May

PRINCIPAL CRAFTSMEN (CONTINUED)

Windows, Zeluck, Inc.

Circular Stair and Other Timbering, Rod Jones of Strong Timbers, Inc.

Stone Walls and Fireplaces, Carston Seales Company

Roof, Traverse Bay Roofing Company and Jake Zimmerman

Landscaping, Traver Wood of Site Planning Devlopment, Inc.

Barn Timber Frame, Rod Jones of Strong Timbers, Inc.

Stone Supply, Brian Fernsemer of Inspiration Stonework

Stone and Tile Work, Waterland Tile, Co.

Stone Work, Keith Szajnecki

Other Builders and Craftsmen, most of the region's finest

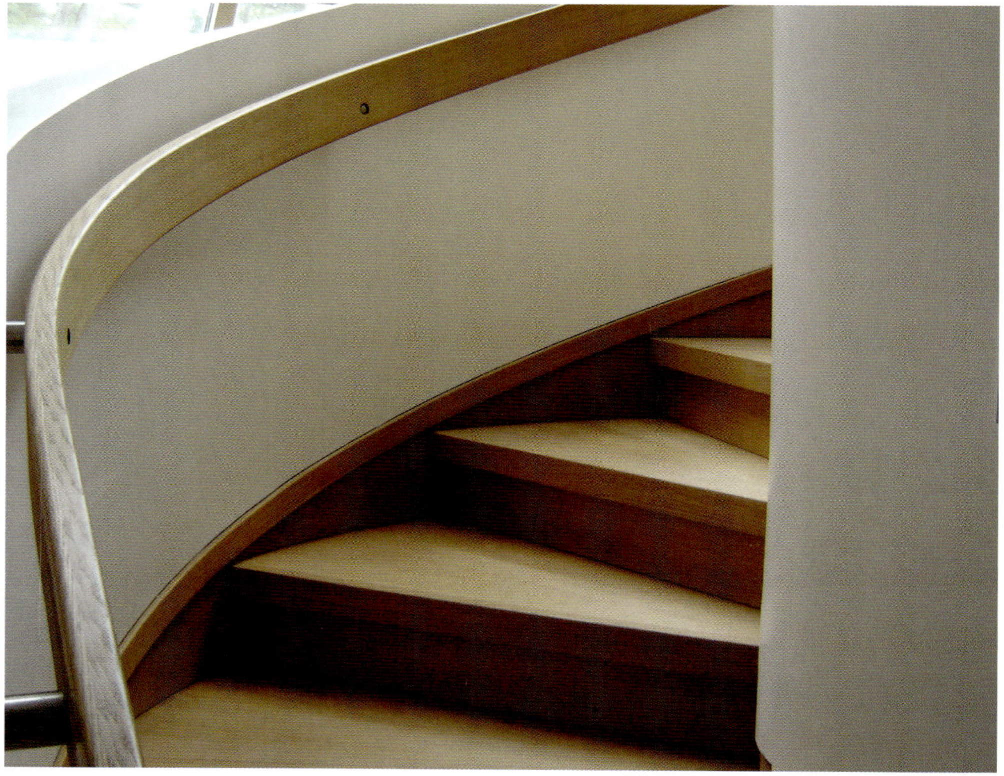

PINE HOLLOW INSTITUTE

Pine Hollow Institute strives to heal people and planet Earth through intelligence, creativity, and compassion.

Founder, Leslie Lee

President and CEO, Dale Hull

10400 South Bayshore Drive, Elk Rapids, Michigan 49629

www.pinehollow.org